Historical Monuments in Hungary

Historical in

Corvina

Dezső Dercsényi

Monuments Hungary

Restoration and Preservation

Contents

* Figures in italics refer to illustrations

PUBLIC BUILDINGS 65

ECCLESIASTICAL BUILDINGS 66

Translated by Elisabeth Hoch
Translation revised by P. M. Clark
Photographs by Lajos Dobos,
Archives of the National
Inspectorate for the Preservation of
Historical Monuments
Map and drawings by
Gizella Bulsievicz
Cover design by Gábor Pécsi

Printed in Hungary, 1969
Kner Printing House, Gyoma

PREFACE

"It is imperative that we preserve and collect the relics of our past before they perish once and for all, or else our past will be the emptier, our present the poorer and our future the less stable." These words were written in 1878 by Arnold Ipolyi, who in Hungary is considered as the first art-historian.

Man is of necessity bound to his past. But as his memory is limited in time and space, he must inevitably resort to national traditions, archives and monuments to discover the meaning of the community he derives from, to carry on the work of his forbears and to set his children's future on a solid foundation.

To conserve the local traditions of a family, village, province or nation, or to preserve the written records relating to the history of a country is a perfectly feasible aim often involving little expense. To preserve historic monuments is an altogether more complex and protracted undertaking, involving detailed planning, but it is nonetheless indispensable, since in themselves traditions and records give only a partial idea of what the nation's life was like in the past.

Historic monuments have in fact a multiple value, the constituent parts of which vary from one to the other. Each represents a particular age, a moment of artistic creation; the finished work, and often individual parts too, can be dated. In studying its historic monuments separately and comparatively, one can follow the evolution of a country stage by stage, its hesitations and its advances, its defeats and its victories—thereby we are confronted with the living forces which have moulded the destiny of a nation.

Thus the siting of a castle like that at Diósgyőr for instance will show us how insecure the region was in different ages, while its position betrays the origin of the invaders it was designed to hold up and its architectural development the importance attributed to it. The richness of its fabric shows the power of its owners and its present condition the political evolution of the country. It is in fact almost a "page" of history, illustrating and complementing data furnished in records and archives.

The walls of a monastery or church abound with similarly precious information on the art and history of Hungary. Every monument surviving to bear witness to an irretrievable past must then be safeguarded; but if necessary it must be restored too, made "articulate" and accessible to all those who feel bound to them by forces which are uncontrollable or difficult to analyse, forces which give a man the feeling of belonging to a well-defined community whose unity has been forged by a common language, artistic traditions and politico-economic interests.

It is thus a national duty, one which Hungary has been aware of for more than a century but particularly in the last two decades, to safeguard the monuments and restore them with the help of the most modern scientific techniques. The country may justly be proud of the results obtained, as they are described in detail in this book.

In recent years however the novel idea has gained ground that the historic past of every country, and in particular its historic monuments, is not solely the property of that country's inhabitants, but forms part of the common cultural heritage of all humanity. In his appeal for the preservation of the sites and monuments of Nubia, Mr Vittorino Veronese said on 8th March, 1960:

"These riches belong not only to the countries which are the depositories of them today. The whole world has an interest in their survival. They are part of a common patrimony which includes the message of Socrates and the frescoes of Ajanta, the walls of Uxmal and Beethoven's symphonies." And his successor, M. René Maheu, the Director General of Unesco, saw in these "precious relics of ancient times a source of joy–'A thing of beauty is a joy for ever'" and in their preservation "spiritual conquest and intellectual and moral progress" (9th November, 1963). This induced him to launch in 1964 an Internatinal Campaign for Historic Monuments, since, he observed, "we realize that the question of the life or death of monuments concerns us deeply, and may be stated succinctly – either we bear in the eyes of the future the culpability for letting a large part of the relics of past civilizations gradually crumble away, and thereby deny future generations the chance to acquaint themselves with the works the past has bequeathed us and which we sacrifice to the enticing speculations of a drunken, overbloated new world that will be the negation of the old; or else we accept the principle of human solidarity in time as well as space and, in a new frame of mind, accept our role in the chain of history, in the knowledge that we live in an age which does no more need to destroy in order to create, which is perfectly capable of including in the most audacious plans for the future a respect for the heritage of the past, and which has the means to facilitate modern man's dialogue with the masterpieces of his forbears."

It will later be seen that Hungary had already adopted the second attitude.

Because there are, there can no longer be cultural frontiers. The great communication routes of the world are no longer the exclusive property of an élite. Every year a host of travellers spreads over the surface of the globe seeking to make contact with neighbouring or less familiar cultures. This seasonal exodus, an increasingly important factor, improves relations and makes for a better understanding between the nations; it is one of the major elements favouring the peace mankind so ardently desires. Hungary was so well aware of this that in May 1966 she played host to Unesco's executive council, which put on the agenda of the 76th session the question of the protection of historic monuments and its relation to tourism. On this occasion the competent authorities offered us a unique opportunity to visit several regions with a wealth of historic monuments. I am thus in a position to bear witness to the importance which the government of Hungary attaches to protecting its historic monuments and bringing out their real value. Anyone who wishes to convince himself of this need only read the pages of this book.

Ali Vrioni
Special Assistant to the Director General of UNESCO

INTRODUCTION

The preservation of historical monuments in Hungary has a history over a century long. The initial steps in this direction were taken in the middle of the nineteenth century, but had to be abandoned after the failure of the 1848–1849 War of Independence, and could only be resumed after the Austro–Hungarian Compromise of 1867. It is nevertheless worth while considering these first efforts, for the intellectual climate of that age had essentially determined the direction followed by Hungarian monument protection for nearly half a century.

On 22 February 1847 the Hungarian Academy of Sciences made a fervent appeal to every Hungarian who had "the honour of the nation at heart" to espouse the cause of the preservation of historical monuments for, in contrast to other nations, "we were indifferent towards our ancient glory and its relics" and had allowed them to decay. The appeal called upon all those who "had the elucidation of Hungary's cultural past at heart and therefore also the improvement of the nation" to report to the Academy all the mobile and immobile relics they knew of. It was probably as a result of this appeal that Lajos Kossuth, President of the Commission for National Defence, issued an order on 30 November 1848 for the protection of antiquities which might be discovered while digging entrenchments. The reason given, that "learning must not be forgotten even in the thick of the fight, for it is our duty to foster it at all times", reveals an interesting facet of the spirit of the 1848 Revolution and the political leader of the War of Independence.

The wave of absolutism that followed the failure of the War of Independence in 1849, gradually thwarted all institutional efforts aiming at the preservation of historical monuments in Hungary; but, in the prevailing climate of intellectual resistance, concern for the relics of national history could only grow. Hardly a year after the fighting had died down, the *K.u.K. Zentral Commission zur Erforschung und Erhaltung der Baudenkmäler* was set up in Vienna, and naturally its scope of authority was extended to the whole monarchy, including Hungary. The Commission, as a matter of course, attributed a secondary importance to Hungarian matters in its Habsburg imperial conception. It was only in 1872, that after persistent efforts, a temporary Commission was eventually formed within the frame of the Hungarian Academy of Sciences to deal with the registration, surveying and maintenance of historical monuments in Hungary. The Commission was also charged with drawing up the Historical Monuments Act. As a result of this work, Act XXXIX, governing the preservation of historical monuments, was enacted in 1881.

The new law was neither better nor worse than other statutes of the age promulgated with similar objectives in view in that it failed to reconcile the inviolability of private property with the preservation of historical monuments, demanded by public interest. Its aims were not achieved, less because of the shortcomings of the law itself, than because of lack of funds. According to the respective stipulations, if the owner could not or was unwilling to maintain the building of historical or artistic interest in his property, the State had either to expropriate it or to strike it from the register of historical monuments. As a direct consequence of these measures, only about fifty buildings had been declared monuments up to 1949, that is, the year the new law was enacted. The other buildings of artistic or historic interest were classified under a different category in respect of which no maintenance obligation had been decreed.

Following the Austrian example, the Historical Monuments Act of 1881 created the National Commission for the Preservation of Historical Monuments; a minor official body was attached to the Commission whose members performed their work on a voluntary basis, and without any remuneration. The National Commission for the Preservation of Monuments was maintained till 1934, when it was reorganized into a more efficient body under the same name.

The greatest difficulty the new Hungarian organization had to deal with was lack of funds. The amount that could be allocated in the budget for the protection of monuments was relatively small. In 1901, for instance, it amounted to 80,000 crowns, which also included office expenses. Considering the condition of the Hungarian monuments at that time, and the urgency and high cost of the restorations required, this allocation was ridiculously inadequate: the restoration of Matthias Church in Buda alone amounted to 2,300,000 crowns, that of the Ják Church to 300,000 crowns, while the restoration of Pécs Cathedral cost 1,800,000 crowns.

In spite of these circumstances numerous restorations had been carried out before the First World War. They were financed both by the religious foundation administering the assets of suppressed religious orders and from a five million crowns lottery loan; the second was also, however, intended to cover the completion of the so-called Basilica (St. Stephen's Cathedral), a church of vast dimensions which was under construction in Budapest at the time.

However, it is not so much the laws or institutions, or the ways of procuring the necessary funds, that mark the history of our subject, as the restorations actually performed, and particularly the principles and methods that were used. This is understandable since the methods of restoration employed, and the general attitude to ancient monuments, as well as schemes for their preservation, are sooner or later bound to bring about the laws and institutions with the aid of which the desired objectives can be attained. Naturally, the methods of restoration employed in Hungary cannot be separated from the outlook that prevailed in the country in the various periods. On examination it will be found that out-of-date procedures were only rarely employed; indeed, more often Hungary was among the first in Europe to introduce advanced methods, some of which are still used today.

If we wish to examine the hundred years of the protection of historical monuments in Hungary in these terms, three different periods can be clearly indicated:

I. The period of restoration "in style", that is, according to the main principles governing the restorations started in the eighteen–sixties, the effect of which could be felt to a certain extent until as late as 1934.

II. The second period, reckoned from 1934 (from the reorganization of the National Commission for the Preservation of Historical Monuments into an efficient body), is characterized by the realization of modern aspirations, which were already in evidence at the turn of the century. However, their full development has been prevented by obsolete laws and unsuitable official machinery.

III. The third period, beginning in 1949, and closely connected with the significant changes in the social structure of the country, opened up new possibilities from the point of view of legislation, administration and restoration methods for the protection of historical monuments on a modern scientific basis.[1]

A Historical Survey

Chapter One
RESTORATION "IN STYLE"
(1863–1934)

At the end of the eighteen-sixties, when large-scale restoration work began in Hungary, the reign of the purists was on the decline throughout Europe, and restoration "in style"—which was more in line with the historical architectural trend of the age—became the method. The two trends cannot, however, be clearly separated, as the purist attitude to style was not fully abandoned. Beyond the eclectic architectural style of that age, this development had its roots in the self-confidence characteristic of the nineteenth-century scientific outlook. It was based on the firm belief that with the means available for design and execution, modern techniques were able to restore or, at times, even to build a truer, more genuine medieval construction than Romanesque or Gothic architecture was originally able to create. The architects advocating this outlook and working on the restoration of Hungarian material came partly from Austria and partly from Germany (like Baron Friedrich von Schmidt who was a Viennese, or August Essenwein who came from Nuremberg) and generally shared views with the Hungarian architects who had studied at the *Technische Hochschule* at Vienna and had become concerned with restoration, such as Frigyes Schulek and Imre Steindl. Attempts at more scholarly work in this field were extremely rare, such as the plans for the restoration of Vajdahunyad Castle by Count Antal Khuen which were thwarted by his early death, or the work of István Möller at Zsámbék and Gyulafehérvár (Alba Iulia, Rumania).

The conception of restoration "in style" and the methods it involved found strong response in Hungarian public opinion, both among the social *élite* which commissioned work and among the rather small community of connoisseurs-scholars and archaeologists. The favourable reception of this trend implies that contemporary Hungarian views concerning historical monuments did not fail to agree with the attitude generally adopted in Europe.

In the *Introduction* mention has already been made of the appeal by the Academy of Sciences, with reference to the "honour and ancient glory of the nation". A few years later Arnold Ipolyi, the learned Bishop of Besztercebánya (Banská Bystrica, Czechoslovakia) and the first major student of Hungarian art proclaimed, in the same spirit, with classical concision: "Let us preserve and collect our relics, lest their irretrievable loss should render our past more void, our present poorer and our future more doubtful." (1878.)[2] Hungarian archaeologists and conoisseurs, but above all the people, awakened to consciousness after long centuries of suppression, wanted visible proofs of their country's earlier heroic glory, sovereignty and greatness in its artistic achievements. The parliamentary report recommending the reconstruction of the Fortress of Visegrád expresses the conviction that "in a few years' time the walls reflected in the waves of the Danube, and the beflagged towers gleaming in the sunshine, would proclaim to the whole world the revival of ancient glory from the nocturnal mists of past centuries". The evoca-

I. Budapest, Meggyfa Street: Roman mosaic, 4th century

tion of past glories and the aspirations far exceeding the economic and political realities of the country gained fresh impetus from the Millennial Celebrations in 1896—the thousandth anniversary of the conquest of the country by the Magyars.

The first restorations were started in this almost universal spirit. Naturally, the work was concentrated primarily on castles and churches: the former received priority as part of the cult of national past, the latter because of the religious need. The restoration of St. Michael's Church at Sopron was the first step, in 1863–1864. Although the technical preparations and the raising of the necessary funds required many years or even decades of preliminary work, two vast restoration projects, both with a symbolic significance, started soon afterwards. One was the restoration of Vajdahunyad (Hunedoara, Rumania), the castle of János Hunyadi and his son Mátyás (Matthias) Corvinus, which recalls the most brilliant period of the Hungarian national kingdom. At the same time, the restoration (in 1868) of the first Hungarian Benedictine monastery at Pannonhalma, originally founded by St. Stephen, the first King of Hungary was begun. The restoration of the Fortress of Visegrád (which, thanks to the building activities of Louis I, Sigismund, and Matthias, represents "in addition to its high value as a historical monument, a testimony to the most glorious period of Hungarian history") did not lag long behind either. The restoration of the Church of Our Lady (better known as Matthias Church) at Buda, and Kassa (Košice, Czechoslovakia) Cathedral, began a few years later in 1873, and were followed by Pécs Cathedral, which was started at the beginning of the eighties (1882). All these works constitute typical examples of the restoration methods of the period.

The story of the restoration of *Vajdahunyad* may be regarded as tragic. The almond-shaped fortification built at Vajdahunyad at the beginning of the thirteenth century was, at the beginning of the fifteenth, bestowed by Emperor Sigismund on the family which thereafter called itself Hunyadi. János Hunyadi, Regent of Hungary and a violently anti-Turkish warlord, began to develop the castle around 1430 and completed the work by the middle of the same century. The castle was further embellished by his son. After the death of Matthias Corvinus, feudal anarchy, the disruption of the country into three parts, and eventually the frequent change in owners during the Austrian rule contributed little towards its embellishment. In 1854 the castle—then the property of the *Bezirksvorstand*—was destroyed by fire; its restoration began as late as 1868 on the basis of very sensible plans designed by Francis Schulz, a pupil of the Viennese architect, Baron von Schmidt. After his early death, the work was, unfortunately, taken over by Imre Steindl with the intention of making the castle look "more beautiful than ever". When Parliament had enough of his extremely costly building and decoration plans, Steindl resigned but the contrac-

II. Feldebrő: Detail of fresco, first half of 12th century

tors continued the work for some time causing severe destruction under the pretext of restoration. It was only in the eighties that the direction of the work was taken over by Count Antal Khuen and, after his death, by István Möller whose activities will be discussed in detail later. By this time, however, the romantic development of the castle had progressed too far to be altogether corrected.[3]

The restoration of the *Benedictine Abbey of Pannonhalma* under the direction of a highly active abbot, Chrysostom Crues had a more fortunate history. It was carried out by Ferenc Storno, who had studied in Landshut and Munich, and in 1863–1864 had been in charge of one of the earliest restorations in Hungary—that of St. Michael's Church at Sopron. The work started with the restoration of the Abbey Church in 1868 (completed in 1875); this was followed by the restoration of the Gothic cloisters (1882–1886.) Storno showed considerable moderation in Pannonhalma, especially in the restoration of the church. While in Sopron he replaced practically every carved stone detail, including the sedilia, by new ones, at Pannonhalma he refrained from making any essential change in the ground plan; he also left the Renaissance and neo-Classical details of the church unaltered and kept even the Romanesque doors of the stairway leading to the crypt—the latter a product of the Baroque period. He did, however, add two side-chapels to the building. According to the custom of his time, however, he removed all the furnishing that was other than Romanesque in style, and replaced it by neo-Romanesque altars, pulpits, etc. of his own design; he also decorated the building with stained glass windows designed by himself. In the view of modern scholarship, the greatest damage was caused by cleaning the stone surface of the walls, since not only may frescoes have disappeared with the plaster, but the whole interior has lost that fine wall texture which is so characteristic of Cistercian workmanship, only to receive instead a stone surface of cold and rigid effect.

With the cloisters, remodelled in the second half of the fifteenth century, Storno acted more freely. While his work on the church could easily be verified on the basis of drawings by Robert Onderka, dating from 1859, the extent of damage in the cloisters was only revealed in the course of the latest restorations in 1961. He changed all the Gothic window tracery and planned Gothic tracery for the arcades which had been remodelled in the Baroque period, for—as he writes—he had "discovered the original form of the Matthiasian* windows". The archaeological research carried out before the latest restoration supplied valuable information on the first, Romanesque cloisters, while wall-exploration work revealed a Romanesque door and brought a further highly interesting result. After stripping the so-called *Porta Speciosa* of the gilding applied by Storno it was discovered that, following the two thirteenth-century building periods, the

* late Gothic, from the reign of Matthias Corvinus (1458–1490)

doorway had been restored during the Baroque period; the work shows little understanding of the original Romanesque form, yet it is evident that efforts had been made to follow it.[4]

The restoration of the *Castle of Visegrád,* originally composed of several buildings, was started in 1871 with what was obviously the oldest part of the monuments, the defence system of the so-called "Solomon's Tower", situated at the most prominent point of the grounds. The building of the mid-thirteenth century keep had been initiated by Maria Laskaris, the Greek Queen Consort of Béla IV, who feared a repetition of the horrors of the Mongol invasion. The core of the lower castle is an elongated hexagon in shape, with late Romanesque and early Gothic elements, and it was designed to control the road along the Danube. The fortification wall surrounding the keep blocks the way from the north down to the Danube, which indicates that it was built against eastern invaders. The wall climbs up to the citadel built on the very top of the hill. The construction of this castle built on an irregular ground plan with an internal tower on the summit of the rock was started shortly after the completion of the keep. The Visegrád Fortress played a highly important role in Hungarian history; it remained a royal residence to the end. From the middle of the fifteenth century even the symbol of Hungarian sovereignty, the Royal Crown, was guarded in its citadel. In the Turkish siege of 1543 the southern corner of the keep collapsed to its base.

In 1871 Frigyes Schulek, the architect directing the restoration, first restored the gatehouse next to the keep, after which he started work on the keep itself. He wanted to build up the collapsed wall with ashlars imitating the original material, and to interspace the large unbroken mass of wall with early Gothic windows. However, he did not succeed in executing his project, for when half of the planned height was reached the work had to be abandoned, and the uncompleted part was temporarily covered by a simple wooden structure. This wooden top was burnt down in 1951, leaving the task of restoration to our generation. Few jobs have posed such a problem for Hungarian restoration experts as that presented by Solomon's Tower. All concerned agreed in that the yawning gap must be closed, but the solutions suggested for this purpose varied greatly.

The continuation and completion of the original plans of Frigyes Schulek after a lapse of eight decades were irreconcilable with present-day outlook. The closing up of the tower with a modern structure (involving the use of laminated reinforced concrete, glass, etc.) would have led the spectator to indentify the structure built by Schulek with the original tower. Finally, the plan suggested by János Sedlmayr was put into practice. It aimed mainly at the reconstruction of the original unbroken bulk of Solomon's Tower, for which, naturally, the use of up-to-date means was foreseen. Before beginning the work, excavations were carried out to throw light on the medieval structure. In the interior of the tower the original wooden beams have been replaced by reinforced concrete ones; only on the top floor, vaulted in the fifteenth century, did the designer try to suggest the original vault by starting out from what remained of its springers.[5]

The building of the *Church of Our Lady* on Castle Hill *in Buda* began in the middle of the thirteenth century. It had a nave and two aisles, but no transept; the nave terminated in a polygonal apse, while the aisles were square-ended. In the second half of the fourteenth century it was altered into a hall church, and the polygonal apses date from that time. In the second half of the fifteenth century, King Matthias adorned the church with a Gothic tower and oratory; hence it is commonly known as Matthias Church.

Up to 1896 Frigyes Schulek, the architect in charge of the restoration aimed, above all, at "extricating" the church from its surrounding by creating an open space around it that could never have existed in the Middle Ages, nor in later times. He thereby reduced the monumental effect of the building which originally rose above small houses; later this effect was practically annihilated by the erection of a neo-Gothic public edifice in the square. (After World War II efforts were made to improve the situation by reducing the height and the exaggerated ornaments of the latter.) Schulek carried out some important changes also in the ground plans of the church. He re-established the thirteenth-century side, pulled down the medieval chapels and created new ones on the opposite side of the church. We also owe him the neo-Gothic decorative elements of the western and southern façades; they culminate in the perfectly new development of the south-western tower. The Romanesque Fishermen's Bastion behind the church is similarly the work of Frigyes Schulek. It now constitutes one of the evocative elements of the Danube view of the capital.

However, Schulek's work is instructive not only as an illustration of restoration "in style", the general practice of his period, but also from the methodological point of wiev, for it clearly demonstrates how the very best intentions may turn to their reverse if the main concern of the restorer is not that of saving the remains of a valuable building. Although Schulek studied the architectural history of the church with scholarly thoroughness and installed copies their original place, the result of his work was only a fascinating but rather bleak neo-Gothic building—especially in its general effect. It is typical of Schulek's methods that in the course of the restoration work carried out after the Second World War, we succeeded in displaying the fragments of a medieval relief found in their original position in the pediment of the southern, Nuremberg-inspired porch, but re-coloured in harmony with the neo-Gothic whole.[6]

When the restoration of *Kassa Cathedral* was started in 1878, the methods employed and the simultaneous case of the reconstruction of Matthias Church in Buda under the pretext of restoration, provoked some animated discussion among the official experts, but a modern scholarly approach did not prevail on this occasion either. The church was reconstructed according to the ideas of the architect Imre Steindl.

The building of Kassa Cathedral, on the site of a Romanesque basilica destroyed by fire, began at the end of the fourteenth century on an early Gothic plan with radiating chapels, a solution rather unusual at that time. The work was drawn out over a long period of time; thus the church itself, completed in the second half of the fifteenth century, already reflects the form and style of the Viennese St. Stephen's Cathedral. The sixteenth- to eighteenth-century history of the Kassa Church records numerous devastations and war damages, yet as one of the most important works of Hungarian Gothic architecture, it was a monument that greatly influenced the development of architecture in Upper Northern Hungary (today part of Czechoslovakia), and Transylvania (today in Rumania). The extremely rich architectural details of its interior, its retables (among them the largest in Hungary), further, its wooden statues, frescoes and fine metalwork have made the monument an unparalleled treasure-house of medieval art.

At Kassa, too, the extremely poor condition of the chancel and southern walls made the complete reconstruction of these two parts inevitable. Dispute about methodological questions broke out in connection with the alteration of the internal spatial arrangement. In the simple-aisled plan the transept running through the second bay from the west created an almost centralizing spatial effect. Steindl was of the opinion that the medieval master mason had in fact designed double aisles but his bungling workmen changed the original plans and built single aisles. Accordingly, he wanted to alter the church into a double-aisled one. The contemporary chairman of the National Commission for the Preservation of Historical Monuments, Baron Gyula Forster, opposed the plan as vigorously as he could and requested the expert opinion of Baron von Schmidt in the matter. Schmidt supported what he called "the archaeological standpoint" of Forster but expressed the surprising opinion that the reconstruction of the three-aisled interior would not cost less than the five-aisled solution. Thus the latter was eventually carried out. However, Forster's view, according to which the southern tower started in the fifteenth century should not be completed, prevailed in the end, and it is also probably due to his influence that the Baroque cap of the northern tower was not altered.[7]

In the last few decades of the century, when the most significant restoration projects were launched, expert opinion was already clearly defined, but it came up against the practice of the established restorers, the masters of historical architecture, and lacked adequate support in public opinion. Thus, the restoration, or rather the complete reconstruction of the Cathedral in Pécs according to the plans of the brilliant Baron von Schmidt was again carried out with official support.

The building of the *Cathedral of Pécs* as a basilica in the Lombard style, with a nave and single aisles, was started in the second half of the eleventh century; its full completion, with the four-towered exterior and extremely rich interior sculptural decoration and paintings, may be put at the middle or, at the latest, at the second half of the twelfth century. The building had no transept; it was provided with a large-size crypt and had a trussed or a flat roof. From the point of view of the later fate of the church these circumstances are of particular significance as the fourteenth- and fifteenth-century vaults have created a situation whose ultimate consequences had to be considered with the restoration of the building.

Still during the Romanesque period, a chapter house was attached to the south-eastern tower of the church, while the episcopal palace practically leaned against its south-western side, thereby greatly reducing the effect of the western main entrance. After the Turkish devastation, the main entrance already opened from the small square on the southern side of the cathedral. It was in the middle of the eighteenth century that the interior was remodelled in Baroque style; this was followed by the restoration of the severely damaged chapter house, which, with the exception of a Romanesque coupled window left unaltered—an unusual circumstance at that time—actually meant the reconstruction of the building in Baroque style. In connection with the foundation work involved, an early Christian crypt was discovered, and the building site was therefore shifted a few meters to the east behind the apses. This solution completely opened up the southern façade of the cathedral which had never been entirely visible during the Middle Ages.

At present, the Cathedral Square in Pécs is one of the most beautiful quiet squares in Hungary. (This was foreseen by the Austrian military engineer, Batschek, who acted as advisor during the restoration work.) Its development actually constituted one of the causes of the complete remodelling performed. Together with statical problems of the structure, in particular the support of the lateral thrust of the vaulting, the demand for a unified façade matching the unified interior of the church, had appeared equally urgent even at the beginning of the nineteenth century. The plans had been worked out by Mihály Pollack, the greatest master of Hungarian neo-Classical architecture, who had solved the problem in a unique way by applying a sham façade of predominantly vertical arrangement, which had also incorporated some Gothic elements. But the building operations carried out between 1805–1827 failed to solve the basic problems, and therefore when the situation gave the reconstruction fresh actuality, the issue of developing the façade and interior "in style" was raised again. Baron von Schmidt, the architect of the Viennese St. Stephen's Cathedral, had first put forward a moderate plan, against which Bishop Nándor Dulánszky, his employer, demanded a "restoration fully in style". The work started in 1882 involved the demolition of the church to its very foundation walls at several points, and also the sale of its Baroque and Zopf altars; only a red marble Renaissance tabernacle, a seventeenth-century Dutch relief and—from the architecture—the crypt were spared. The laying of the foundation stone in 1883 was celebrated with great solemnity. Schmidt demolished a great part of the walls and planned a Tuscan Romanesque basilica on the Zara and Pisa models; however, in designing the most accentuated element of the church, namely the sham southern wall, he was guided by the basic principles of Mihály Pollack's plan, rather than by the models previously mentioned. This shows that his basic idea was an impressive, unified appearance—unbroken even by the four towers.

Baron von Schmidt observed, assessed and recorded the data bearing on the Romanesque basilica, and stored the covered stones with scrupulous care and scholarly accuracy; the greater part of the latter he replaced by newly carved copies to which he gave their original function. (Thus he commissioned György Zala with the modelling of the reliefs in the stairway leading to the crypt.)

The reticence shown by the experts of the period constitutes a much discussed point. True, Baron Gyula Forster raised his voice for the preservation of the original internal arrangement of the cathedral in 1885, when the work at Pécs was already in progress, but the literature on the subject—though it admits that full reconstruction had been carried out—appears to have found nothing exceptionable in this solution. In 1894 Péter Gerecze, the Cathedral historian and a member of the National Commission for the Preservation of Historical Monuments, wrote the following: "Schmidt had solved his big and difficult task as a whole as well as in detail in the best possible way, both from the artistic and historic points of view of our days."[8]

The alterations foreseen in connection with the restoration of the Cathedral of Pécs met with extremely unfavourable responses in non-professional public opinion. Immediately after the first presentation of the plans, a priest called Alajos Garay pleaded for the preservation of the earlier building, and the local papers printed statements which severely condemned the "restoration".

Although the controversy elicited by the restoration of Kassa Cathedral had failed to prevent the planned alterations, the fact that a dispute broke out about them indicates that the revision of the earlier views on restoration methods was gaining ground both among laymen and experts. It is due to these circumstances that, for example with the restoration of the Ják Church (1896–1904), restoration executed with a meticulous care unusual for the period took the place of the type of the alterations we have just described.

Ják: The portal of the Benedictine Abbey Church before restoration

III. Feldebrő: Detail of fresco, first half of 12th century

The *Benedictine Abbey at Ják* was founded around 1220; its first period of construction was interrupted around 1240 and the Abbey church was only consecrated in 1256. It is a basilica, with a nave and aisles but no transept, the aisles terminating in semi-circular apses. It represents one of the most advanced examples of the usual family-founded church-type in Hungary that have come down to us; its elaborate sculptural decoration makes it a monument of European importance. At the time of the Mongol invasion (1241–1242) the façades of the church with their characteristic Norman Bamberg ornamental motifs and the richly decorated main doorway, common also in Lower-Austria, stood fully completed. In the interior, the typical ornament of family-founded churches —the seigniorial tribune spanned between two towers, and the elaborate projections of the vaults, a feature of Cistercian architecture, were also ready, but not the vaulting. It appears that the northern aisle was vaulted in a primitive way before 1256, while the southern aisle and the nave were covered with a flat wooden ceiling evidently destined to serve as a temporary covering.

The restoration of the church, severely damaged by Turkish attacks and by lightning, began according to the plans of László Gyalus in 1896, and was completed in 1904. Although it involved the demolition of the tower walls down to the second floor, and the stone tower caps copied from the Zsámbék church to replace the original ones considerably altered the proportions of the towers, no essential change had been made in the layout or size of the building. The severely damaged stones were replaced, but the substitution was carried out without causing a break in the ornaments. This method was also followed in the case of the main doorway. However, the apostle heads whose originals had been destroyed by the Turks but were later replaced by Baroque ones, have been left unchanged while the head of Christ and that of four of the apostles are still original Romanesque work. The most important change was carried out in the interior of the church where the two aisles were covered by cross-vaults, as originally planned; the profiles of the original ribs of the porch and those of the square sanctuary bay were used for this purpose. As medieval stone carving techniques could not be imitated by modern methods, the parts replaced by the restorer are distinguishable even now.[9]

The example of Ják clearly demonstrates that the trend in monument protection advanced towards more scholarly methods; radical reconstruction performed under the title of "restoration in style" met with increasing resistance on the part of both laymen and experts.

It has been mentioned already in the *Introduction* that, in addition to the romantic efforts at recalling the glory and art of the past, scholarly considerations began to play a part at an early date, as in the order issued by Lajos Kossuth in 1848. The formulation of the principles of modern preservation of historical monuments and, in

IV. Veszprém: Fresco in the Gisela Chapel. Detail. 13th century

some instances, even their practical application, took place before the close of the nineteenth century.

In connection with the restoration of Kassa Cathedral we have already mentioned the views professed by Baron Gyula Forster, Chairman of the National Commission for the Preservation of Historical Monuments. He based his outlook on the knowledge of modern Austrian and French trends, which he not only advocated in theory but strove to follow in practice. In his important work *(Legislative Protection of Historical Monuments in Hungary and Abroad)* published in 1906, he analyzed the deficiencies of Hungarian legislation and, dwelling upon the principles of restoration, made the following statement: "The task we are confronted with is not one requiring the architect to demonstrate his genius and fantasy by remodelling and reconstructing our historical monuments; it demands far more. Through an intimate knowledge of their style, he should endeavour to protect and preserve them with loving care in their original form, with every respect for the spiritual work of the original architect." In a further passage he writes: "What right has the restoring architect to consider, say the thirteenth-century parts of a historical monument, as the original structure, and to destroy the rest because it is the product of the fourteenth, fifteenth or sixteenth century, or to keep only those parts that, in spite of his suppositions based on the thirteenth-century work, he decides to leave unaltered?" Forster severely condemns the destruction of the original surroundings of monuments for the sake of spatial background, and cites the Church of Our Lady (Matthias Church) on the Castle Hill of Buda as a warning example.[10]

The principles advocated by the Chairman of the National Commission for the Preservation of Historical Monuments were put into practice by the architect István Möller, with the preservation of the Zsámbék ruins. Like the church in Ják, the *Premonstratensian monastery at Zsámbék* was a family foundation. It was also a three-aisled basilica without a transept, with a pair of towers on its western façade, and a tribune inside; however, early Gothic elements replaced the rich late Romanesque forms. The main chancel had a polygonal ground plan and the lateral thrust of the cross-vaulting was supported by flying buttresses located in the loft above the aisles. In the fifteenth century the monastery belonged to the Paulite friars; in 1763 it was partly demolished by earthquake. The work of preservation began in 1889 under the auspices of the National Commission for the Preservation of Historical Monuments.

The parish of Zsámbék had a Baroque church, thus ecclesiastical requirements did not interfere with the principles of restoration. The Commission also gave the architect a free hand to carry out his own ideas. Möller considered it his most important task to preserve the existing parts of the monument; he only completed its structures in places and to an extent absolutely necessary for their protection, and even used a contrasting material for this purpose.

We believe that the preservation of the Zsámbék ruins was a precedent of considerable significance for restoration specialists in Hungary, since it proved that only what is regarded as the modern "archaeological outlook" permits the preservation of a building without necessarily requiring its reconstruction. However, in addition to the methodological interest, great importance is attributed to the work done at Zsámbék, because it constitutes the first example in this country where a medieval ruin was preserved by modern technical means, instead of it being rebuilt "in style". As far as we know, similar preservation work was still rare in the whole of Europe at the end of the nineteenth century.[11]

István Möller also directed the restoration of the *Cathedral of Gyulafehérvár*. The Cathedral has preserved numerous architectural styles beginning with the late Romanesque period. In the thirteenth century it was a basilica with a nave and aisles, a transept, a square tower and two further towers flanking the open porch on the western side. Although the layout was based directly on French prototypes, its essential features were already known in Hungary at that time; the Lombard and Norman details, on the other hand, connect the Cathedral with the principal example of Transdanubian Romanesque architecture, the Royal Palace of Esztergom, and with the family-founded monasteries. The devastations of the Mongol invasion were hardly repaired when in 1277 the Cathedral was plundered and set on fire. The two documents on its restoration—actually two employment contracts—are among the rare relics of the medieval building trade in Hungary. The restoration was followed by the extension of the chancel in early Gothic style, after which the Cathedral—which became a symbol of Transylvania—was developed further in practically every century; thus, its tower is built in Gothic style, and the chapel added later is a fine piece of Renaissance architecture.

Because of lack of funds, Gyulafehérvár Cathedral hall escaped restoration "in style", only its walls had been strengthened but, unfortunately, the plastering of the walls had been removed and the stone surfaces were renovated. In 1904 István Möller continued the restoration. He endeavoured to establish the Romanesque situation by excavations, and replaced only those of the ashlars which had become useless, not omitting to mark the new ones with his initials and the date of replacement. Although owing to the outbreak of the First World War the restoration of the Cathedral could not be finished, the work Möller accomplished until then may be regarded as exemplary in its way.[12]

Naturally, World War I caused a break in the restoration work which was by then advancing along healthy lines, for with the development of hostilities all restorations in progress had to be abandoned. The Revolutions which followed the war in Hungary, and in particular the Hungarian Republic of Councils (1919), immediately tried to introduce organizational changes: it dissolved the National Commission for the Preservation of Historical Monuments with the intention of setting up a more efficient body. Unscholarly methods which, under the title of restoration, have deprived many a building of its original form, ranked among the principal reasons given for the dissolving of the Commission. The Cultural Commissariat demanded the drafting of a new bill for the protection of historical monuments, and started the cataloguing and, in the most important cases, also the surveying of the existing material without delay.[13]

After the fall of the Republic of Councils the situation in the field of the preservation of historical monuments was critical. Hungary lost about two-thirds of her former territory under the Peace Treaty of Trianon, and these border regions mostly involved areas which had never been reached by the Turks, and, as such, were far richer in historical monuments than the central portion of the country. Financial ruin, retaliations following the revolution, and—last but not least—the re-establishment of the National Commission for the Preservation of Historical Monuments, all but caused the decline of this important cultural field. After the fall of the Republic of Councils the Commission had to be re-established, for its dissolution was the work of the defeated regime. Under these circumstances, a solution to the problem could no longer be sought in the formation of a more modern body. The experts in favour of up-to-date principles were divested of their offices for having participated in the reorganization of the Commission; those who remained at their posts supported the old outlook. The subvention received by the Commission was so limited that it would not have sufficed for the restoration of a single building, still less for the completion of the works started during the war. This stagnation lasted till 1934, when Professor Tibor Gerevich, the art historian of European renown, was appointed Chairman. After a short trial period Gerevich reorganized the Commission into an efficient body, without altering its name, and recalled its former technical director, Kálmán Lux, into office. Further, he obtained considerably larger restoration funds and thus started a new era of development in a difficult cultural and economic situation. Preservation of historical monuments in Italy played an important role in the ensuing progress, especially from the technical point of view, for Gerevich enjoyed friendly relations with the Italian experts. Moreover, most of the Hungarian experts of historical monuments had been trained in Rome or pursued post-graduate studies there.

Chapter two

PROLOGUE TO THE MODERN ERA (1934–1949)

The short period of fifteen years during which the reorganized National Commission for the Preservation of Historical Monuments continued to operate, involved not only large-scale excavations, but also the introduction of up-to-date techniques and theories. Progress had been greatly hindered by the lack of a register of historic monuments therefore work was started along two paths. The first undertaking aimed at the detailed systematization of the existing historical monuments by individual regions, the other at the preparation of a small topographical survey of the historical monuments following the system of the Dehio-lists, which was to give a short description of all historical monuments in the country. Of the first project, the first volume, covering the Esztergom collections, appeared in the period under review; the latter, small topography was published at the beginning of the following period.

The obsolete Historical Monuments Act now presented a hindrance to development, and therefore a new Bill was drafted in which the Italian and French experiences of historical monument protection were considered. The Bill did not come up for debate during this period but it was enacted—if with certain important changes—in the period that followed.

The cause of the preservation of historical monuments in Hungary was most effectively advanced by four important excavations and by the exhibition of their results on the site. Hungary is extremely rich in archaeological finds, and widespread excavations had been carried out earlier to reveal the relics of, and obtain information on, the culture of the different periods, from prehistoric times to the foundation of the Hungarian State. However, Hungarian medieval and Renaissance architecture have not been so well treated. Although it had been suggested earlier in various writings on the subject that the gap which a century and a half of Turkish occupation had caused in Hungarian art history should be filled by the systematic excavation of our monuments of medieval and Renaissance art, it was only after the sensational results of the Esztergom excavations, which aroused great general interest, that these suggestions were followed up.

The site of a few thousand square feet on top of Esztergom Castle Hill, an elevation practically surrounded by the Danube, had also played a significant role outside the scope of Hungarian history. The Romans, who came in the wake of the Celts, built the *castrum* of Solva on this site; later, Slavs, and after them Hungarians, settled within the Roman walls, as on many other places along the Danube. The easily defendable position of Esztergom made it a suitable place of residence for Prince Géza, the paramount chief of the Hungarian tribes in the second half of the tenth century. It was here that King (Saint) Stephen I was born, and at the beginning of the eleventh century the palace and cathedral of the Archbishop of Esztergom were built. Because of the leading role secured by the Archbishop towards the end of the twelfth

Esztergom: Section of the Royal Chapel after restoration

century the royal and thus also secular centre of the country became a centre of the Catholic Church. At the beginning of the thirteenth century the Court was transferred to Óbuda, after which Esztergom developed into an episcopal town and the royal palace situated in the grounds of the castle was also ceded to the Archbishop. The castle and St. Adalbert's Cathedral were added Gothic and Renaissance parts. In 1543 the Turks occupied the castle and the town, and held them, with only short interruptions, until the end of the seventeenth century. During this time the see was at Nagyszombat (Trnava, Czechoslovakia) and it was transferred to Esztergom again only at the beginning of the nineteenth century, at which time the building of the biggest neo-Classical cathedral in Hungary was started. What concerns us most in this connection is that, for the sake of the new cathedral which was to stand on the medieval site, the builders reduced the ground level by 25 to 35 feet, destroying to the very foundations the medieval and even the Roman buildings. In 1934, when excavations began in connection with the reinforcement of the fortification walls, results of interest were anticipated only at the southern corner of the castle, where the ground level had not been changed. Work at this spot shortly revealed a red marble stairway leading to the core of the Romanesque castle; a chapel, and a door to the palace opened from its small landing. The walls of the chapel, decorated with splendid Trecento frescoes, were found standing taller than those of the palace, but big pieces of the latter—one of them still showing a Renaissance fresco—were also still extant. It was furthermore established that the Romanesque hall, already known, with a vault supported by a central column, had also belonged to the palace. Excavations carried out during the past years have revealed at about the same level the remains of the eleventh-century palace which preceded that of King Béla III (1173–1196) in particular the foundation walls of a large-size chapel of circular ground plan.

The excavation and restoration of the Palace of Esztergom which was completed in 1938, is still considered as the highest standard of work of its kind both on account of the technical expertise employed and the very effective way in which the finds have been presented to the public.

The palace had been severely damaged, probably by the siege of 1596 and its collapsed vaults were found lying on the floor of the halls. It may be assumed that, instead of reconstructing the building, the Turks filled it up from wall to wall with earth to form a strong bastion in the direction most exposed to attacks. By doing so, they preserved the ruins of one of the greatest works of medieval Hungarian art for our own age. The restoration has been carried out by various methods depending on the condition of the material brought to light; in some cases the fragments could be replaced without anastylosis, in others they required completion, the extent of which was naturally determined by the quantity of the material found. The dimensional effect of the chapel could be re-established completely, and the amount of the unearthed rib fragments and wall columns permitted the unequivocal identification of the original system of the vaulting. As far as could be followed from the frescoes and mural paintings, the original ashlars were put back in place; in other parts the missing stones were replaced by small-size bricks specially manufactured for this purpose. With the aid of a reinforced concrete ceiling hidden in the loft of the chapel, most of the ribs could be fixed in their original position.

In two other halls the wall columns and the vaults could not be reconstructed with similar certitude; they were, therefore, covered with simple reinforced concrete roofing which gives the halls an almost museum-like appearance. At the lower levels the excavated walls did not require any completion.

The excavation and restoration of the Castle of Esztergom were carried out by the architect Kálmán Lux under the direction of the Prelate, Antal Leopold; there is no doubt, however, that credit for the consistent application of strictly scientific methods is due to Tibor Gerevich.[14]

Apart from the Palace of Esztergom, another great Hungarian early medieval centre which has been excavated is the Basilica of Székesfehérvár. Esztergom was the centre of the State and Church in the early Middle Ages, while Székesfehérvár, and the cathedral within it, was the cultural centre of the Árpád dynasty. The place maintained its function even under later dynasties, up to the Turkish occupation. Most of the Hungarian kings were crowned and buried in the Székesfehérvár Cathedral. Though some of the chapels were still in usable condition after the expulsion of the Turks, the ruins of the building were razed to the foundation walls in the Baroque period to give place to the new episcopal palace. It was only by mere chance that in 1839 a tomb, presumably that of King Kálmán (1068–1116), was found.

At the beginning of the War of Independence in 1848, János Erdélyi and subsequently Imre Henszlman carried out excavations in Székesfehérvár, the latter on three occasions. Only the tomb of Béla III and his wife could be identified among the many tombs revealed besides the foundation walls of the cathedral. The verificatory excavations performed in 1934–1938 failed to trace even part of the previously excavated walls. The remains of the building have, therefore, been embedded in green grass, for exhibition in a garden setting; a large quantity of carved stones are displayed in a *lapidarium* adjoining the excavation site, and the coffin of Stephen I, carved from a Roman sarcophagus, is kept in a separate building. Thus Székesfehérvár, the coronation and burial town of Hungarian medieval kings, regained the monuments of its early history, if only in the form of an open-air museum and *lapidarium*.[15]

V. Ják: Fresco, mid-13th century

The third big excavation was performed in Szombathely, on the site of the ancient colony of Savaria, founded by Emperor Claudius (41–54 A.D.), where an important public building of the Roman town was revealed, richly decorated with mosaic. Its Roman foundation walls, discovered accidentally in connection with the extension of the episcopal seminary, were excavated by the archaeologist Stephen Paulovits. Later the finds were conserved and displayed according to the plans of Kálmán Lux. At that time it was still believed that the building—which terminated in a semi-circular apse on the western side, but bore the marks of different periods and was richly adorned with mosaic in the Aquileian style—was identical with the basilica figuring in the Quirinus Passion and supposed to have been raised over the resting-place of the martyred Bishop* of Szombathely. More recent investigations have shown, however, that the ruins unearthed are those of an imperial palace erected on the site of earlier structures. In addition to the foundation walls and the splendid mosaic ornamentation, the excavations revealed some impressive remains of the Roman road system. The garden setting in which the finds are now exhibited is broken only by the buildings protecting the mosaics.[16]

The excavations carried out at Óbuda (Aquincum) resulting in the partial restoration of the military amphitheatre, were designed to display a similarly impressive Roman building. The oval-shaped amphitheatre, measuring nearly 100 yards across, was excavated between 1935 and 1940. Its restoration and exhibition have been solved by the architect, László Gerő, in a most ingenious way. In addition to preserving the ruins, he has reconstructed two axes of the walls at points where the building has perished completely. The work is a fine early example of preservation combined with interpretative exhibition.[17]

Finally, in the period under review, the excavation of the Royal Palace at Visegrád was begun, bringing highly significant results.

Visegrád has been discussed in detail earlier in this study in connection with the restoration of the so-called Solomon's Tower. Under the reign of Charles Robert, of the Neapolitan House of Anjou, when Visegrád was the centre of the Hungarian State for a few decades, a royal palace was erected there on the bank of the Danube. This building, practically completed between 1320 and 1335, was extended by Louis I (1342–1382) who succeeded Charles Robert on the throne and was later restored by Sigismund, King of Hungary and Holy Roman Emperor (1387–1437). It was finally turned into a Renaissance palace by Matthias Corvinus. The palace was severely damaged under the Turkish occupation, after which most of its remaining structures became covered with earth washed down from the hill by torrents of water, the

*Saint Quirinus, Bishop of Siscia (third to fourth century A.D.)

VI. Sopronbánfalva: Fresco in the Church of Mary Magdalen. Detail. 14th century

surface remains being used for house building by Bavarian settlers.

For various reasons, we have seen, the quiet village had drawn to itself the attention of Hungarian archaeologists and restoration experts for nearly a century. The description, however, of the 350-halled royal palace by Miklós Oláh, Archbishop of Esztergom (1493–1568) was almost unanimously considered to be an example of the exaggeration of humanist court historians. Only János Schulek, son of the restorer of Solomon's Tower, kept searching almost fanatically for the site of the palace, until he eventually discovered it on New Year's Eve, 1934 when he found the springers of a barrel vault in the wall of a local garden. He rightly presumed this vault to be part of the support of the huge main staircase figuring in Oláh's description. His assumption was later confirmed by his own excavations, and by those of several others in later years. During the first days of his work he found the chapel and excavated the court of honour which had formed the centre of the palace, and the so-called Hercules Fountain, a red marble Renaissance structure in the centre.

The excavations, continued with modern archaeological methods after World War II, have partly clarified the extent and building periods of the palace. According to our present-day knowledge, the complex consisting of three units was terraced into the hillside to make the most of the natural features of the ground. The most important building, probably the King's residence, was separated from the Queen's wing by a chapel. The Renaissance staircase mentioned before led to the terrace with lime trees in front of the chapel, situated at a higher level. Today the chapel and most of the royal palace are almost fully unearthed but only a small part of the queen's apartments has so far been excavated.

The excavations and restorations carried out at Visegrád during the past three decades give a clear picture of the development of methods of preservation in Hungary. The excavators of the first period were mainly interested in unearthing architectural and archaeological finds; later the excavations were performed with a view to investigating, with the whole arsenal of modern techniques, the various layers of the ruins, and the sequence of building periods to which they belonged. In addition to elucidating the architectural history of the palace, this work resulted in the excavation and restoration of two large and splendid fountains. The excavations showed that Chimenti Leonardo di Camiccia, the Florentine architect employed by King Matthias, united the 1,900 foot long, at certain points multistoried, palace complex by a single, grand staircase. His work demonstrates the co-existence in Hungary of two apparently conflicting styles: the Gothic and the Renaissance, whose simultaneous cultivation was, however, characteristic of the country's architecture. The arcaded galleries surrounding the quadrangular court of the King's wing were Gothic, following the style of the cloisters of the Middle Ages; their masters are

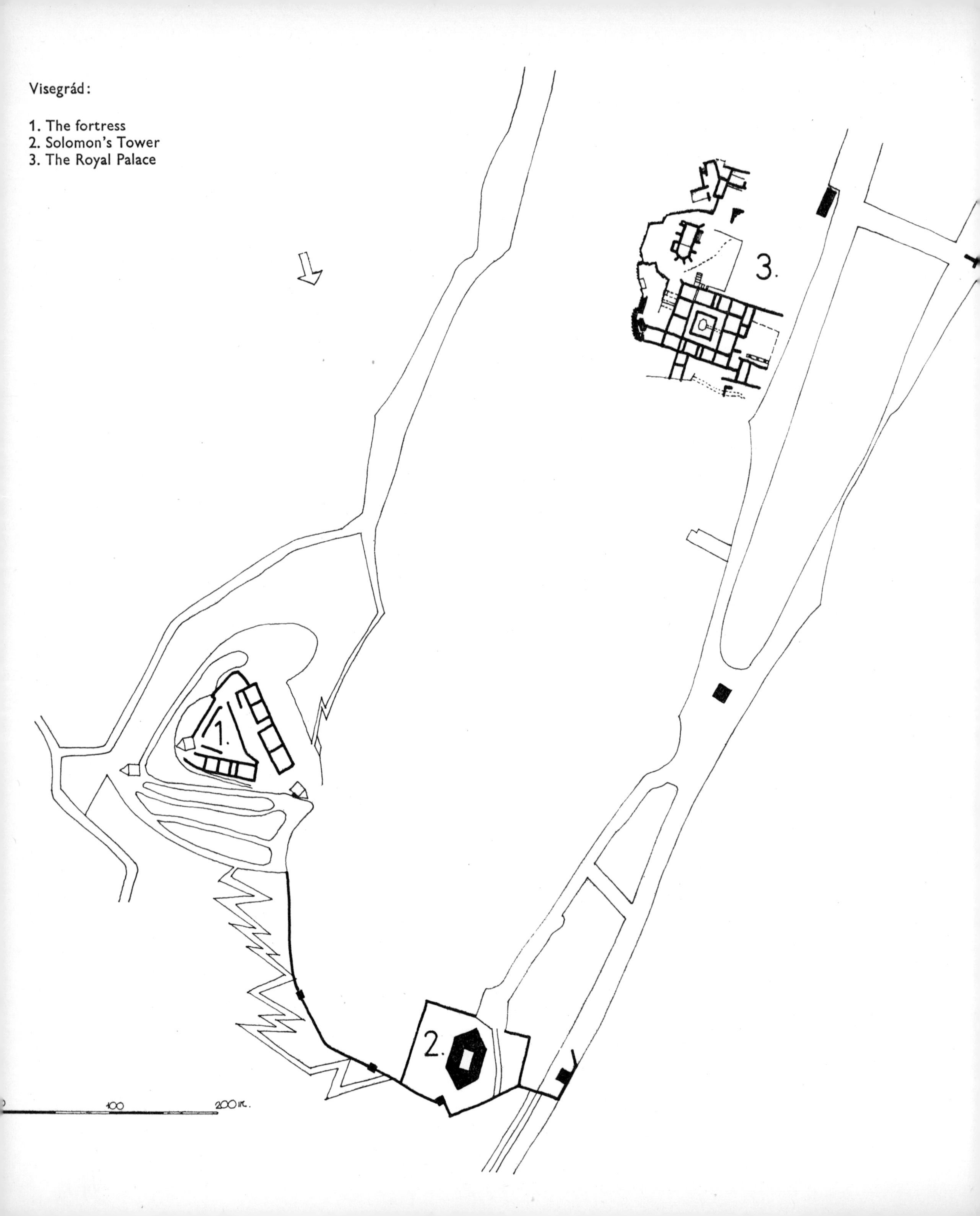
Visegrád:
1. The fortress
2. Solomon's Tower
3. The Royal Palace
1.
2.
3.
100
200 m.

known to have built the cloisters of Fazekas Street Church at Kolozsvár (Cluj, Rumania), and the Benedictine Monastery at Pannonhalma. The court of honour was at the same time adorned with a red marble fountain reminiscent of the finest Florentine work. Whether it is the work of Giovanni Dalmata, who was engaged by Matthias Corvinus, or that of Tommaso Fiamberti, the so-called "Master of the Marble Madonnas", or of both, is open to question. Galleries adorned with a Renaissance-style balustrade and pilasters ran above the arcaded court. According to our present knowledge, it was mainly the ornamental elements (such as the fountain of the court of honour, the red marble segmental pediment of the chapel, and the tabernacle carved from Italian white marble) which were executed in the Renaissance style. At the same time, the second fountain, built to replace the former Angevin one bearing the family arms of Matthias and adorned with lions, is still pure Gothic in its conception.

As has already been mentioned, the results of the excavations have been exhibited in different manners at different times, as attitudes to scholarship and restoration techniques changed. They all had, however, one basic feature in common, in that, beyond ensuring the preservation of the historical monuments, they had recourse to reconstruction only in a single case, with the one gallery of the arcaded court, and with the two fountains mentioned earlier, where archaeological data and the imposts and other fragments found on the spot enabled this to be done authentically.[18] Otherwise, the palace was unearthed in a state of decay which ruled out the reconstruction of its halls, and only the conservation and presentation of the existing walls could be considered. The standard procedure employed with the Royal Palace of Esztergom could not be used at Visegrád, for here the walls of the earlier buildings built of ashlars had been replaced by the plaster-covered brick walls of Sigismund and Matthias. The first attempts at restoration consisted in raising the existing walls slightly in height and covering them with pebbles for protection; in later experiments the decayed structural cores were completed with brick. The result, however, was the production of large-size, monotonous, brick-red geometric forms in the field. We now build the complementary protective walls of stone, and the addition appears some 15 to 20 centimetres above the wall to be preserved, the level of the original wall being marked by the interpolation of a row of red bricks, according to the usual practice with the conservation of ruins.

Among the many measures taken for the preservation of historical monuments during this short period of fifteen years, we ought now to deal at some length with that concerning the preservation of mural paintings.

At one time it was believed that medieval and Renaissance mural painting in this country was insignificant both quantitatively and qualitatively, and that this branch of painting had developed only during the Baroque period when the best Austrian masters worked in Hungary. Up to 1934 the restoration of murals was unfortunately entrusted to poorly trained, rather amateurish painters. However, the preservation of the Trecento and Quattrocento frescoes discovered at Esztergom required special skill, not only in view of their unparalleled value for Hungary, but especially because they had been buried in damp earth until their excavation. The work was carried out by one of the most outstanding Italian restorers, Mauro Pelliccioli and his colleagues, with the help of young Hungarian restorers. After Esztergom, Pelliccioli restored the murals of the Ják Church, and also cleaned and conserved those of the Roman Catholic parish church of Sümeg. The latter contains a series of frescoes by Franz Anton Maulbertsch, the greatest of all Austrian Baroque painters. Although the pictures covering the whole church belong to his early period, they display his finest qualities. György Kákay Szabó, one of the Hungarian pupils of Pelliccioli, restored the late fourteenth-century murals by János (Johannes) Aquila in the small church of Velemér, and uncovered the frescoes of the high altar of Vác Cathedral–also a work of F. A. Maulbertsch–which had been immured at the end of the eighteenth century, while Ferenc Deed restored the mid-thirteenth-century murals of the so-called Gizella Chapel at Veszprém, and the twelfth-century frescoes of the Feldebrő undercroft.

The old church of Feldebrő is an enigmatic monument and the source of much debate, so that the art-historical problems associated with it need mentioning here. The first and most interesting church was built probably in the eleventh century and was an ambitious monastic central-plan building with terminal apses on at least three sides and measuring some 20 x 20 metres. Whether the interior plan was an inscribed Greek cross or in fact had a longitudinal axis of nave and single aisle is a matter of debate, although the side-apses suggest double aisles. Underneath the two most easterly bays was an apsidal undercroft containing some fine eleventh-century frescoes in the Byzantine style and reached by stairs from the outer aisles. In the thirteenth century, probably during the 1241—1242 Mongol invasion, the upper church was largely destroyed, and when it came to be rebuilt in the following decade or so, the impoverished population built a simple, aisleless Romanesque parish church with a single eastern apse using the material from the ruins. The old side-walls were pulled down and used to fill the arches of the nave, so that a much narrower building resulted. The undercroft was reached now through new steps down from the nave, and the old steps now outside the walls were filled in with rubble. During the Turkish occupation this church also became ruinous, and so a new, rustic Baroque church was erected incorporating the old, but adding an extended east end and a western tower. Excavations and wall-examinations have revealed the ashlar walls, nave piers and foundations of the eleventh-century central church. The finds have been protected by retaining walls. The frescoes of the groin-vaulted undercroft were restored by János Illés in 1961–2. On this occasion further frescoes came to light and the iconographic program of the crypt was also elucidated. It centered around two subjects: the Pantocrator enthroned in the glory of the new Jerusalem, and the origins of the Eucharist in the Old Testament.[19]

Chapter three

THE PROTECTION OF HISTORICAL MONUMENTS AFTER WORLD WAR II

At the close of World War II, when the whole country had become a battlefield, two types of buildings suffered especially heavy damages: dwelling houses and the palaces and country mansions of the nobility. The historic quarter of Buda, and the Royal Palace itself, were in ruins. About twenty of the houses regarded as historical monuments were completely destroyed, and in fact not one of the 200 that had been considered as such actually survived the war intact. Most of them suffered severe, rather than slight damage. Although the devastation in the inner, historic parts of the towns of Sopron, Győr and Székesfehérvár were not quite so disastrous, the losses in historical monuments were also heavy in these areas. The castles and manor houses—buildings marking the eighteenth- and nineteenth-century style of life in Hungary—usually stood in small village settlements. When the front line drew near, the owners deserted these country seats and even if the latter escaped direct war damage, they were often plundered and damaged by the local inhabitants. The substance of the buildings thus left unused for years deteriorated rapidly; their 150- to 200-year-old timbered ceilings decayed all the more rapidly since already the financial circumstances of the owners during the inter-war years hardly allowed them to think of carrying out essential renovations. Although considerable progress have been made in this field since the war, the restoration and renewed utilization of the castles and manor houses in question still represent one of the ma-

jor problems in this country. The damage in ecclesiastical buildings was fortunately less extensive.
The reform of the organization responsible for the protection of historical monuments, and that of the relevant laws, took place as early as 1949, after the consolidation of the political and economic situation. From this is clearly demonstrated the importance the Government had attached to this question. Decree 13 of 1949, regulating the Museum Affairs and the Preservation of Historical Monuments, was among the first enacted after the Presidential Council had recommenced its activities. It was naturally based on the bill prepared before the war, but was completed with new provisions adopted from the respective laws in force in the Soviet Union. It decrees that the maintenance and restoration of historical monuments is incumbent upon the owner (the greater part of the buildings was in fact at the time of enactment already in public property) and invests the newly established National Centre for the Maintenance of Museums and Monuments with legal authority to appraise the restoration plans from the point of view of the preservation of historical monuments.

Essentially, the new organization assumed the character of the body the Hungarian Republic of Councils had planned to set up earlier, with the propitious additional feature that the organic connection established between museum affairs and the preservation of historical monuments permitted the centralization of the relatively limited number of experts and the utilization of their work in both fields. Although the National Centre for the Maintenance of Museums and Monuments functioned only for two and a half years, its activities comprised numerous enterprises to which we will revert later; we should first like to review the development of the present situation in respect of organization and legislation.

After the dissolution of the National Centre, the protection of historical monuments came within the terms of reference of the then newly established Council of Architecture; later it was transferred to the National Buildings Committee, which remained in charge until 1957, when the National Inspectorate of Historical Monuments was formed, acting under the control of the Ministry of Works. (In 1967 the scope of authority and the name of this ministry was altered to the Ministry of Works and Urban Development.) in Hungary the whole building trade, including the building material industries, comes under the control of this ministry. The protection of historical monuments is thus under the control of an essentially industrial ministry, instead of a cultural portfolio, as is usual throughout Europe, as well as in socialist countries.[20]

This solution was chosen because it was believed—and this assumption have been corroborated by the experience of the past fifteen years—that more effective provision can be made for the preservation of historical monuments within the frame of town development plans than in isolated projects for their maintenance or restoration. Regional plans are designed to make use of the potential of a larger economic unit or, occasionally, of a tourist trade centre, and to make recommendations for its development. In tourist centres—which will be discussed in detail later—the restoration of historical monuments offers vast possibilities, whether the buildings are exploited in a direct way (as hotels, restaurants, coffee-bars, etc.) or whether they attract the visitors in their own right as historical monuments. The use of such historic buildings or building complexes can be determined within the framework of the detailed development plans of the individual areas beforehand. The plans for environmental development ensure the role of the historical monument within its urban surroundings and thus provide also for its physical and visual presentation. It is hardly necessary to add that projects for monument preservation involving whole towns—and this type of planning has increased in importance since World War II—can only be realized within the framework of regional and detailed development plans. Thus the close connection formed between the protection of historical monuments and urban development, and the united control exercised over these two spheres of activity, produces definite advantages. This is true not only from the point of view of the historical monuments, but also from that of urban development, for monuments of architecture are suitable for illustrating both the history and the main stages of urban development of an area over a long period of time. Another reason for bringing the preservation of historical monuments under the works portfolio was that the administrative activities connected with the former were the concern of the local building authorities. In view of these circumstances, it appeared that the authority concerned with monument protection should be responsible to the ministry which controls the building authorities and urban development, and this attitude has now been fully justified.

Today buildings listed as historical monuments (representing Category I) figure in development plans as items to be maintained under all circumstances. A further resolution orders the preservation of buildings of some historic or artistic value and those of townscape value (Categories II and III) provided they can be economically included in the appropriate development plan. In practice, this means that historical monuments are to be included in the development plans as a given factor, whereas the fate of buildings belonging to the lower categories is decided during the course of the preparation of the plans.

However, since the preservation of historical monuments is primarily a matter of cultural policy, Hungarian laws ensure that, regardless of the departmental responsibility for its implementation, the influence of the Ministry of Education should be allowed to prevail in several respects. First of all, inclusion in or exclusion from the

VII. Esztergom: Fresco in the Royal Chapel. Middle of 14th century

list of historical monuments; further the determination of protected areas (protected towns) require the agreement of the Ministry of Education. The utilization of historical monuments for cultural purposes also comes under the aegis of this ministry.

Naturally, the concept just described in broad outline has been incorporated into the country's statutes, as a result of long years of legislative work.[21]

The statutory provisions referred to above are based on the fundamental principle that "historical monuments, their environment, and all works of fine and applied art associated with them, represent irreplaceable relics of the country's past", and their preservation is therefore of public interest, for the sake of which the rights of the owner or user may and, if necessary, should be curtailed. (At this point it should be mentioned that the protection of objects of artistic value not associated with a given building is provided for by the Museum Law.) The ministerial preamble emphasized in this connection that "In Hungary the preservation of historical monuments is of greater significance than in any other European country. A great part of the material have been destroyed by disastrous wars, and therefore those which have survived must be granted increased official protection." For the implementation of this principle "external or internal renovations, restorations, alterations, extensions or demolitions, or any other work affecting the character or artistic appearance of the building in any way; in addition, the determination of, or changes in, its use, are subject to the respective instructions and preliminary agreement of the Minister". (This right has been transferred by the Minister to the authorities concerned specifically with the preservation of historical monuments.)

In the Building Act *historical monument* is used as a generic term; the decrees issued for the enforcement of the law specify, however, the various categories of protection granted. According to these "historical monuments are irreplaceable relics of the country's past; they represent material evidence of the country's economic, social and cultural development and are of outstanding significance from the point of view of its architecture, history, archaeology, fine arts, applied arts and ethnography."

The specification of *buildings of some historical or artistic value* (Category II) is similar to the above, with the difference, however, that instead of "outstanding significance", the term "importance" is used.

"A building is of *townscape value*—whether in towns or villages—if in view of its lesser historical or artistic interest it cannot be listed as a historical monument or as a building of some historical or artistic value, but owing to its external appearance it still plays an important part in the formation of the characteristic aspect of the town."

The last-mentioned category may be unusual in European practice, since the buildings involved have no special historical or artistic value. However, they do play an

VIII. Esztergom: Fresco in the library of Bishop János Vitéz, second half of 15th century

important role in the traditional Hungarian townscape. The statutory provisions protect only the outside appearance of these buildings. Moreover, in principle, they may even be demolished, if according to the judgement of the authorities responsible for protection the building destined to replace the existing one is capable of the same part in the townscape or even to improve it.

The terms Class I, II, III, etc., current throughout Europe in the classification of historical monuments are avoided in Hungarian usage because they may lead to the underestimation of the lower categories. Naturally, our own grouping also represents a certain order of value, which is significant from the point of view of the extent of the protection to be granted. For the sake of convenience, however, we shall occasionally revert to using Categories in the present book.

"*Protected areas* are such contiguous parts of an area which illustrate the historical development of a characteristic settlement pattern (the linear pattern and development of its squares and streets), further, such urban districts, squares, streets, or sections thereof, where buildings listed as historical monuments, buildings of monument character and buildings of townscape value form a unit or a characteristic townscape."

By *environment of historical monuments* such "architectural and scenic environments are understood which ensure the appearance and undisturbed effect of a historical monument".

A few statistics will be quoted in an attempt to give an idea of the amount of buildings affected. For the sake of comparison we should mention in the first place that at present altogether 2,500,000 buildings situated in 68 towns and 3,178 villages are being kept on record in Hungary. These figures include certain sections (generally the centres) of 13 towns which are designated as protected areas; 1,867 buildings and structures are registered as historical monuments whose protection extends to contiguous sites (publicly owned land) in accordance with the ministerial decree cited before, unless the areas involved had been scheduled for separate protection (which has occurred in about 100 cases so far). The number of buildings in the second Category is 5,869, while that of buildings protected for their townscape value amounts to 1,285.

According to the law, the maintenance and restoration of historical monuments invariably devolves on the owners or (if in State property) the users, who in case of failure may be compelled by the authorities to meet this obligation. Buildings without owners or unsuitable for use according to their original purpose (e. g. castles, ruins, etc.), or those whose restoration the owners are unable to cover from their own resources (e. g. churches, rural houses, etc.), are restored partly or fully against centrally issued preservation grants which are administered by the National and Budapest Inspectorates of Historical Monuments. The National Inspectorate is responsible directly to the Ministry of Works and Urban Development for its activities, while the Budapest Inspectorate discharges its duties within the framework of the Budapest City Council, as part of its Building and Urban Development Section. The National Inspectorate of Historical Monuments exercises technical supervision over the Budapest Inspectorate so that a uniform administrative practice may be developed, and views on the preservation of historical monuments may be consistent over the whole country.

As the Budapest Inspectorate of Historical Monuments discharges its functions in the capital, it may come to depend more firmly on the support of State-owned building companies (first of all, the designing offices and contractors of the capital itself). However, the Inspectorate has a small-scale designing office, and a section for the restoration of murals, under its own control. Most of its grants are used for the restoration of houses but all churches scheduled as historical monuments (77 in number) and the most important ruins (e. g. Aquincum, the excavated ruins of the capital of the Roman province) are also being gradually restored.

Owing to its wide range of duties, the National Inspectorate of Historical Monuments is a more complex organization. Matters of administration are dealt with by a special section which also controls the social organizations and the so-called sub-committees for Historical Monuments. The same section is responsible for information and publicity.

Great importance is attached to basing the preservation of historical monuments on the widespread support of both professional circles and the lay public. On the professional level, various committees serve this goal such as the Committee of Historical Monuments, acting within the Association of Hungarian Architects, the Committee of the Hungarian Academy of Sciences for Theoretical and Historical Research in Architecture, the Hungarian National Committee of ICOMOS,* and the Committee of Historical Monuments acting in an advisory capacity for the Ministry for Building and Urban Development. In these, the best Hungarian experts (architects, archaeologists, and art historians) discuss specific restoration plans, as well as theoretical problems.

The Research Section of the National Inspectorate is primarily concerned with research work on particular historical monuments. Most of the restorations carried out by the National Inspectorate require excavations or the exploration of walls in order that the history of the building may be retraced with the help of archaeological data and physical examination, to complement the information provided by the few available written sources. A number of workshops concerned with the restoration of objects of art including workshops for stone and for wood carving employing large staffs, and a few specialists in the restoration of murals, are also attached to the Re-

* International Council of Monuments and Sites

search Section. This section is also in charge of the publication of scholarly proceedings and the preparation of popular scientific books and pamphlets.

The almost one-hundred-year-old Hungarian organization for the preservation of historical monuments owns some very important collections. These are handled by a special section, which controls the library, the archives, the collections of photographs and the photographic laboratory. The Collections Section has also been entrusted with the organization of a Hungarian Museum of Architecture.

The greater part of the restorations carried out from the funds of the Inspectorate are planned by the architects of the Design Section, and are executed through Project Branches, operating under the control of the Building Section. At the present time seven such branches (with head offices in Budapest, Eger, Nyíregyháza, Pécs, Sopron, Székesfehérvár and Szombathely) employing a permanent staff of about 650 people, are working at 65 to 70 different sites a year. They carry out special tasks with the help of skilled workers acquainted with the building techniques of past ages. The organization also accepts orders from outside commissioners if restoration work requiring special skill is involved. The annual value of the orders thus received is about equal to, or slightly exceeds, the own funds of the Inspectorate.

It follows from the foregoing that the architects on the staff of the Inspectorate deal mostly with the conservations of ruins or restorations involving special tasks. Thus they are concerned, not only with designing, but also with the detailed scholarly elaboration of the restorations executed and with the extensive study of problems of technique. When, on the other hand, restoration or construction in a protected area is initiated by an outside body or by local government, drafts and recommendations for architectural solutions supplied by the architects of the Inspectorate help considerably in taking the decisions in which the demands of the Inspectorate and utility are reconciled.

The policy followed in connection with the preservation of historical monuments during the past decades has centred around three main points.

In the first place, the types of structure eligible for preservation had to be decided and an inventory of the protected items had to be published, as only in this way could the building authorities be successfully drawn into the work envisaged according to the respective law. Scientific and popular scientific studies on our historical monuments had to be published. Restoration methods had to be developed and elaborated in appropriate detail, not only for the buildings but also for objects of art. Finally, a scheme for the selection of the objects of restoration had to be worked out, as the financial means, building capacity, etc. of the country required the rational concentration of resources. The greater part of all these tasks have been accomplished during the past ten years.

The cataloguing of historical monuments started soon after the enactment of Act 13 in 1949, but the completion of this work required a survey of the whole material in Hungary. The Small Topography compiled according to the Dehio method appeared in 1951,[22] but it does not nearly contain a complete list of the buildings and monuments deserving protection. The tracing and registration of these took place through the so-called "Townscape and Historical Monuments Investigations".

The planning and execution of this work was the first important advance since the coordination of our activities with urban development, for, like so many others, the respective studies were originally carried out for the preparation of urban development plans. Every Hungarian town was studied from the point of view of its historic buildings and general appearance, and an inventory and short description of the historical monuments deserving preservation were drawn up. The surveys were generally made jointly by an architect and an art historian, and were also documented by maps and photographs. In addition to the inventory, the material so prepared in each case included both general recommendations and specific advice on the solution of preservation problems and the improvement of the given townscape, and this has been of great value to the local authorities, who in many cases adopted and executed the plans suggested.[23]

This cooperation between the two branches resulted in the publication of the first provisional list of Hungarian historical monuments in 1960. It contained, in topographical order, all items under protection in the country. The revision of the list started immediately after its first appearance, since up to then only the items listed as historical monuments could be surveyed on the spot. This surveying work was completed in 1969, and the final list will soon be published.

In addition to the compilation of the List, the Inspectorate has devised serial publications both for narrowly professional purposes and for the wider public. The first of these, the so-called Great Topography, gives a complete inventory of objects county by county, together with the history of each settlement within the given area, a list of literary sources, a description and illustrations of the local buildings and other monuments, as well as the technical and photographic documentation and bibliography of the more important items. They naturally cover both mobile and immobile objects and thus also constitute the most important works of reference on Hungarian art history. A nouvel feature of these volumes is that, in addition to an introduction on the art history, they contain a chapter on the history of the archaeological material of the respective county. Eight volumes of the series have been published so far.[24]

Beside the full topographical series requiring longer preparation, a series of monographs have been published on the more important historical towns. They contain an introduction dealing with the cultural history of the respective town, a description of its historical monuments and an analysis of its areas of 'townscape value'. The twenty-four volumes which have appeared to date cover practically every town possessing historical monuments of importance. Finally, to meet the demands of the wider public, the series entitled *Our Historical Monuments* and *Our Restored Historical Monuments,* containing the description of individual building of architectural and historical interest, have been published cheaply in large numbers.[25]

Apart from these three types of inter-related work, a quarterly review launched in 1957 and entitled *Műemlékvédelem* (Preservation of Historical Monuments) provides information on current work, while methods of restoration and scientific results are reviewed in a biannual publication.[26]

It has been pointed out in the preceding chapter that the restoration carried out under the direction of the National Committee for the Preservation of the Historical Monuments since 1934, and above all, the restoration of the Esztergom Castle, have provided Hungarian experts with methods which may be definitely regarded as modern and scientific. Naturally, this legacy had to be developed, for the large-scale restoration work started in the second half of the fifties raised a whole series of theoretical and technical problems and called for the elaboration of the principles which, as far as possible, were to provide guidance to designers and contractors.[27]

Hungarian experts are of the opinion that it follows from the nature of historical monuments that other aspects such as their aesthetic value have to be subordinated to historical authenticity from the point of view of preservation. The architect directing the restoration should act as a preservationist whose creative personality must yield to that of the earlier master, that is, he must concentrate his efforts on protecting the work of his predecessor. The same is also valid for the restoration of objects of art. This has been a fundamental principle in the work of the past few decades. A second, hardly less important principle is, however, that a restoration is meant to impress the spectator, usually a layman. Therefore the mode of presentation has to be 'evocative', that is, with the help of scholarship and data, the building in its restored form is interpreted in a way enabling the spectator to experience the impression it had created in its original state. However, interpretative additions may only be used to an extent that will not overshadow the importance and priority of the original parts.

The consistent implementation of this dual principle presupposes reliable knowledge of the architectural period or periods of the building involved. Therefore, in the case of pratically all pre-eighteenth-century buildings restoration is preceded by excavations, so that absolutely authentic data concerning the architectural history may be obtained such as the original delineation of the walls and the chronology of successive rebuildings. The object of this research work is not the restoration of the original or any other interim state of the building at the expense of subsequent details. It belongs to the historic character of a building that it is extended or provided with new furnishings or ornaments during its existence. The real task of the architect consists precisely in deciding from the results yielded by the research and supported by archaeological and historic documentation what the reconstruction should display to the spectator. Although there have been some exaggerated attempts at presentation, in most cases it has been possible to reconcile the historic and aesthetic claims, so that the restored building should present a balanced and harmonious whole and not a historic pastiche illustrating each period of its construction.

Anastylosis is only used in cases where, in addition to the replaceable original building material, the carved details may also be authentically restored to position. We believe that this problem, in the same way as the completion of decayed or destroyed elements (for example, the reconstruction of a number of axes of a nineteenth-century building) is a matter of proportion between the old and the new: the extant parts should always outweigh the newly added structures, and the balance must never shift in favour of the latter.

It is evident from what has been said so far that in Hungary, the preservation of the extant historical monuments is considered as the proper domain of restoration activity; in this view to undertake the restoration of completely destroyed buildings would amount to straying into forbidden fields. This attitude has been formed as a result of many years of debate, and of the practical problems that arose after the Second World War in connection with the use of newly vacant lots. No destroyed historical building has been rebuilt in its original form in Hungary, although the architectural surveying of a good many residential houses on Buda Castle Hill has fallen to our share. It would have been regarded by the responsible experts as falsification, since present-day building techniques cannot produce a fully authentic copy (or if they could, the falsification would be the more complete). Moreover, the newly built "historical monuments" would only have damaged the authenticity of extant ones. Heavy as the damage was in most of our towns of historical interest, the number of buildings completely or almost completely destroyed was not important in proportion to those which survived or which could be restored. Many of our experts wished to solve the problem presented by the gaps in the rows of houses by filling them with undistinctive buildings in keeping with their surroundings. In a few instances such plans have actually been carried out. However, such a solution was to underrate the achievements of modern town planning and architecture. A third course was adopted soon, namely that of commissioning progressive architects for plans up-to-date in conception, yet in keeping with the historical monuments in the given environment. The history of town building shows that it took many generations to develop systematically sited and constructed towns. In every period architects have added to the existing towns items in the style of their own time; it would be wrong, therefore, to interrupt the course of this evolution just as it would not be justified if our own generation failed to cope with its task of erecting new buildings on the sites left vacant by the ravages of war. In such instances, therefore, the National Inspectorate only requires the new plans to conform to the building line and division of sites prevailing in the given street, and that in terms of its scale the new building should fit in with the surroundings (in respect of the height of the building, type of roof, and so forth). We do not interfere with the design of the façade. Some very good solutions have been produced in this way, with some less happy exceptions where the architect had failed to adapt his building to its surroundings in a satisfactory way. The conclusion seems to be that for new buildings erected in a historical environment, architectural and artistic considerations are of paramount importance. A good architectural conception will naturally include adaptation to the given environment.

According to the provisions of the Historical Monuments Act, the protected towns are regarded as evidences of town development and urban history, and not just as a collection of individually valuable buildings. Consequently, it is the most important task of the Inspectorate to preserve the structural pattern that the protected town has acquired in the course of time; this applies not only to the pattern of streets and squares, but also to the smallest unit: the individual site.

Finally, it should be mentioned among principles of restoration in Hungary, that protected towns (or parts of towns) are considered as living organisms, and are therefore not treated as reservations or museum-like protected areas. The historically valuable and, therefore, protected area should be organically united with, and form a living part of, the whole town, with modern dwellings, a network of shops, public institutions, and the like.

To achieve this aim, the detailed development plan of the protected area must be coordinated with the respective general town development plan and, through the latter, with the regional plan. The only difference between the plans for protected parts of towns and those for the town as a whole is that in the former case the problems are worked out more elaborately. Accordingly, they contain details not figuring in other plans, the type of pavement envisaged, the plans of smaller establishments, and especially all the existing and planned streetscapes.

Naturally, traffic also represents a problem in Hungary, although owing to the special features of town development characteristic of the country, part of the protected sections of towns can be excluded from heavier traffic (as in Veszprém and Kőszeg), ot they are provided with

IX. Nógrádsáp: Fresco, 14th to 15th century

a network of sufficiently wide roads (like Buda and Vác). The complete banning of motor traffic has only been necessary in a few places like Sopron, while in towns like Eger where the importance of through traffic did not allow this solution, the traffic has been diverted through a tunnel, in this case under the castle hill.

In addition to the detailed development plans, restoration plans are worked out for every protected town. They determine the sequence of the envisaged restoration, and thus coordinate the research work of art historians with the design and execution.[28]

In restoring works of art, the most important thing is to preserve their substance. Where completion appears necessary, as in the case of mural paintings, it should be carried out at a deeper level in a different colour or form. In the case of the preservation of stone sculpture Hungary is unfortunately in a very difficult position, since the country's climate (under which thaw and frost may alternate in winter several times a day) combined with the destructive effect of polluted air in the bigger cities, attacks the statues and carved ornaments of the buildings most severely. Unfortunately, in Hungary, as in other European countries there is no effective method that would prevent the ensuing damage.

It will be readily appreciated from the preceding account of the development of preservation principles in Hungary that the National Inspectorate was pleased to sign the *Venice Carta* in 1964. It was felt, with some justice, that in knowledge of the principles of the *Athens Carta* and the Italian *Carta del Restauro,* Hungarian specialists had followed the course laid down in the new document for quite a time before its appearance. In 1965 the Hungarian Academy of Sciences discussed the application of the Venice Carta to Hungary at a very fruitful conference which resulted in the publication of the fundamental principles of architectural restoration in Hungary.[29] The policy, expounded above, regarding the restoration of protected towns is also based on the achievements of international conferences, as well as on our own practical experience. At the beginning Hungarian preservation policy had a rather improvising character, since the decayed state of the historical monuments, in addition to the damage caused by World War II, exceeded by far the funds available for restoration. Moreover, the organization then in charge of historical monuments was inadequate for the formulation of a comprehensive plan for the whole of the country. With the formation of the National Inspectorate of Historical Monuments, the basis for the preparation of the necessary long-term plan was established. According to the first draft, a region (the environment of Lake Balaton), a town (Sopron), and a building of paramount significance (the former Royal Palace in Buda) represented the main tasks, besides which, however, restoration work was started at a number of historical monuments whose special value or advanced stage of decay called for early action.

X. Velemér: Fresco, 1378

As has already been mentioned, our regional projects include plans for the development of tourist centres and holiday resorts, with a bearing on the preservation of historical monuments. So far three such regional projects have been completed and submitted to the Government, namely those of the holiday resorts of Lake Balaton, the Danube Bend, and the western Transdanubian region, all of which involve the restoration of a considerable number of buildings of architectural and historic interest.

The region of Lake Balaton, and especially the northern shore of the lake, is rich not only in beauty spots, but also in relics associated with several thousand years of culture. In addition to the Roman *castrum* at Fenékpuszta (Mogentina) villas with mosaic decoration and mural paintings (Balácapuszta) and a ninth-century Slav fortification and church (Zalavár) have come down to us in this area. Among the early Hungarian settlements the most outstanding ones are: the Benedictine Monastery in Tihany, the provostal church in Felsőörs, and, among the village churches, the church of Egregy. From the Gothic period, ecclesiastical and secular buildings—the Roman Catholic Parish Church at Keszthely and a house in Alsóörs—as well as numerous ruins of other buildings of architectural and historic interest (Nagyvázsony, Sümeg) form part of the architectural heritage in this region. From the Baroque period, the church of Sümeg has been included in the plan primarily on account of its mural paintings by Maulbertsch, and so have been the former Jesuit churches in Balatonkeresztur and Vörösberény which are just as rich in mural decoration, although not of the same high quality. The Baroque and neo-Classical styles are represented in the region also by a considerable number of villas, manor houses and cottages, cellars and press-houses. The Lake Balaton preservation plan covers a number of items outside the region proper, as they form excursion centres for people spending their holidays at the Lake, and thus attract considerable tourist traffic.[30]

The regional plans for the Danube Bend have been prepared with similar objectives in view. They, however, cover much larger areas of similar architectural and historical interest and involve even greater tasks of preservation. The right bank of the Danube having been the Roman *limes*, several *castra* and *burguses* have also been excavated in this section. With some exaggeration we may say that at the beginning of the Middle Ages, the area surrounded by the Danube Bend formed a sort of Hungarian *Ile-de-France,* containing many royal residences (Esztergom, Dömös, Visegrád, Óbuda). The most important historic fortresses (Esztergom and Visegrád) together with the most valuable Renaissance remains (the Bakócz Chapel at Esztergom) and Baroque ecclesiastical and secular buildings forming contiguous protected sections in Esztergom, in Szentendre and Vác have come down to us in this region. Among them, the Serbian Greek Orthodox churches of Szentendre, the early neo-

Classical cathedral with frescoes by Maulbertsch in Vác and the biggest Hungarian neo-Classical church, the Cathedral of Esztergom, are of outstanding interest.

The most recent regional plan to be adopted is that covering the western Transdanubian area which is perhaps the richest of all in historical monuments. The so-called *amber road* running through this region had already been one of the most important trade routes before the Roman conquest; thus Savaria (Szombathely) and Scarabantia (Sopron) which are situated along its course have become towns of major significance in the province. (Their centres, together with that of Kőszeg, are now protected areas.) However, while Sopron and Kőszeg had been important settlements as early as the Middle Ages, Szombathely flourished in the eighteenth century when it became an episcopal seat. The finest and most stately Hungarian edifice of its kind, the Esterházy Palace at Fertőd, and a number of other mansions and manor houses of lesser interest, are situated in this area; further, some delightful Hungarian rural buildings have come down to us in the environment of Lake Fertő and also in the southern part of the region.

In addition to these three regions of tourist interest, the restoration of three further highly important protected town districts is now in hand during the current period (1966–1970). These are the residential district on Castle Hill in Buda, and the centres of Sopron and Eger. After World War II the civil settlement and the Royal Palace on Castle Hill in Buda still preserved some precious documents of the capital of medieval Hungary, if most of them only in ruins. The Fortress of Eger witnessed one of the victorious chapters in the war against the Turks, and the episcopal town developed around it represents some of the finest of Hungarian Baroque architecture. Both being important tourist centres, they occupy a prominent place in our reconstruction plans.

However, the fact that all these towns and regions are receiving top priority, does not mean that no restoration work is being carried out in other parts of the country. It only shows that, with a view to promoting the home and foreign tourist trade the Government urges not only the construction of hotels, restaurants, baths, and so on, but also the restoration of buildings of artistic and historical interest within the respective development plans. Close relations between tourist policy and the preservation of historical monuments are required in the first place by the comparatively large internal tourist traffic of the country. The number of Hungarian visitors paying admission fees in the Fortress of Eger is between 400,000 and 500,000 a year; if we compare these figures with the 800,000 or so visitors counted at Pompeii, and consider the foreign tourist traffic of the two countries and the historical and artistic significance of the two places we can only draw the conclusion that it is the large proportion of home visitors that increases the tourist traffic to the above figure at Eger. Similarly, between two and three hundred thousand tourists visit the Royal Palaces of Visegrád and Esztergom every year.

We are very pleased with these developments since one of the primary objectives of the preservation of historical monuments is that the people of the country for whom the work is actually intended should become acquainted with the relics of their own history and art. Moreover, this state of affairs creates favourable conditions for specialists, as an understanding and appreciative public opinion is the soundest basis for their work.

The close connection between restoration and the country's tourist traffic, manifesting itself both in our current work and long-term programme, account for the fact that we welcomed with the greatest pleasure the Budapest session of the Executive Board of UNESCO in the Spring of 1966, which dealt specifically with the association between the preservation of historical monuments and tourism. Apart from listening to the lectures delivered, participants also had opportunities to visit restored historical monuments in the region of Lake Balaton and the Danube Bend,[31] thus gaining a fair view of the significance of the preservation of historical monuments in the development of holiday centres.

Restoration Projects in the Present

In the previous chapter, we have only discussed modern principles of restoration and protection in Hungary in general, together with their legislative foundations and administrative organization. But restorations usually raise peculiar problems whose solution requires the whole range of techniques at the specialists' disposal. In the following the most important projects of the last twenty years are described. The most suitable course of description was offered by grouping the restoration work according to the type of building involved.

THE PRESERVATION OF RUINS

The course of Hungarian history is marked by the devastations of wars. In 1241–1242 the three- or four-hundred-years-old country was ravaged by the Mongols who destroyed all the works of Romanesque art that came their way. The Gothic and Renaissance buildings fell victim to the Turkish occupation of 1541–1686, while those which survived, and the examples of Turkish architecture were swept away in their turn by the large-scale building activity of the Baroque, Counter-Reformation period. In 1702, during the war of independence lead by Prince Ferenc Rákóczi, the Austrians blew up all the Hungarian fortresses, and the ravages of World War II caused heavy damage to our mansions and castles. Thus the number of recorded ruins in Hungary is extremely high (242 buildings and castles in the first category and 168 in the second). As a matter of course, the preservation and presentation of ruins has gained considerable importance.

It has already been mentioned that the conservation of the ruins of the Zsámbék Church, performed by István Möller at the end of the last century, gave a new impetus to work in this field. Indeed, the same principles were observed in the thirties with the conservation of the open-air lapidarium at Székesfehérvár and Szombathely and with the military amphitheatre of the Romans in Buda.

Since almost all that has come down to us from Roman public buildings, dwelling houses and fortifications, is their foundation walls, their conservation and exhibition present a special task. The simplest solution is to preserve the ruins or surviving artistic details by erecting a protective building above them. In Aquincum, once capital of the Roman province of Pannonia and now part of Budapest, the foundation walls of a house and a bath were discovered at 63 Korvin Street while laying the foundations of an appartment building. By altering the plans of the new building, the ancient walls and finds could be displayed on the spot *(Military Camp Museum)*.[32] A special prtective building had to be erected above the house of a distinguished Roman personage, discovered in *Meggyfa Street,* in order that its splendid *mosaic ornaments* would be preserved and exhibited in a way worthy of its value.[33] A fine example of preservation and presentation on the site is the extensive field of the ruins of

Aquincum, where but a few protective layers of stone above the ancient walls and, at certain points, *anastylosis* were used by the designer with the aim of giving the spectator the impression of architectural space at least at some parts of the field.[34] The *Cella Trichora* in Óbuda was preserved in a similar way, but here a contrasting stone material was used for the protective layers covering the remaining walls to show the different periods of the building.[35]

There are other items worth mentioning in connection with the Roman relics of ancient Pannonia (now called Transdanubia or Western Hungary), such as the recently excavated painted crypt in Pécs which has been covered with a protective building; further, the remains, found in the Fenékpuszta *castrum,* of a large store-house and the so-called Basilica II, believed to have lasted from the fourth century to the end of the Slav epoch; and the ruins of the Tokod camp, the walls of which have been preserved by protective layers of stone.

The presentation of the *Szombathely Temple of Isis* and its sacred enclosure is a unique experiment. The temple was probably destroyed by the earthquake of 455 A.D. In addition to its foundations, some splendid white marble reliefs on the main cornice of the building have also come down to us, and the architect commissioned with the restoration made an attempt at displaying the excavated fragments in their original functions, and set up part of the completed columns of the sacred enclosure. The schematic presentation of the façade, and the reinforced concrete used for this purpose, exclude any possibility of misunderstanding, and have permitted a solution which could alone give the layman an idea of the dimensions of the original Roman structure.[36]

Most of the medieval ruins are ecclesiastical buildings; the earliest among them is the so-called *Récéskút Basilica in Zalavár.* This was formerly believed to be a ninth-century church constructed by the Slavs. But more recent excavations have proved that the Récéskút Basilica is a Hungarian construction while the church of the Slav Prince Privina, of about the same size, must have stood on the same spot but its remains lie beneath those of the later, Hungarian structure.[37]

In the preservation of antique and medieval ruins, excavations are always carried out to establish the original situation and to obtain a sounder architectural and historical basis to work on. In most instances they have brought to light architectural remains and objects, besides providing the data required for restoration (the original ground level, for example). The excavation of the *ruins of Balatonfüred Church,* for instance, gave highly instructive results, for it revealed that walls of Roman villas are lying not only beneath the apse of the Gothic chancel, but also beneath the rest of the ruins and their surroundings. One of the excavated graves contained a Romanesque guilt bronze cross, a rare find in Hungary. The restorers' work in Balatonfüred involved more than just the preservation of the church walls, for the finds and the stone material also enabled the restoration of the tribune, characteristic of the family churches of the period. This, together with the remaining walls, gives the spectator the impression of an enclosed space.[38]

The excavation of the remains of another *church, at Alsódörgicse* near Lake Balaton, revealed a double church of the Romanesque period, of which there had been no intelligence.[39] Nearby, the *ruins of the church at Ecsér* (a village destroyed in the Middle Ages) have also been preserved. It was a large basilica with a nave and two aisles, enclosed by an outer wall. Close to this church we struck the foundations of a three-roomed house which may have been the parson's dwelling.[40]

A good example of modern principles of conservation is provided by the *Paulite monastery in Nagyvázsony*. Situated in a picturesque forest clearing, the walls of the former church and cloisters, standing now at various heights, present an evocative picture of ruins integrated with their environment.[41] We had recourse to the erection of a protective building in only one case—with the preservation of *St. George's Chapel in Veszprém*. The small thirteenth-century octagonal chapel stood on the site of an earlier, likewise central structure, built around 1000 A. D. It was, therefore, considered best to cover the whole ruin with a modern protective building which permitted the presentation of the surviving structures without any alteration.[42]

CASTLES

The remains of castles and fortresses rank high among Hungarian historical monuments. To prevent the liberation movements from using them as a base, the Emperor Leopold ordered them all to be blown up in 1702. Since then their ruins have been exposed to gradual decay, for—with the exception of Visegrád and Vajdahunyad—the "restoration" of castles was not even thought of during the past century. Their remains are, however, a testimony to the constant struggle for freedom implanted in Hungarian tradition. They were also the places where our sixteenth- and seventeenth-century culture evolved. It was therefore felt that their excavation and restoration was in a sense an obligation. This work involved the clarification of numerous technical problems.

The true situation regarding the history of the construction of the castles could only be established by archaeological methods, because descriptions, inventories, or other records, which might provide valuable information on the state of buildings at a given date, were rarely found as dating earlier than from the seventeenth century. Generally speaking, the excavations have supplied numerous architectural and historical data and, just as important, have revealed large quantities of material remains on the basis of which fourteenth- to eighteenth-century culture, and most branches of the contemporary applied art, are now seen in a new light.

Through their situation in the different layers of the ruins, the vast amount of excavated art treasures naturally helped to elucidate the architectural history of the structures involved. Thus, the chronology of the construction and development of our castles—of which little was previously known through the lack of artistic evidence—can now be very accurately worked out at several places.[43]

However, the results obtained by research work provided no more than a sound basis for the restoring architect to work on; the technical questions presented by the restoration of the excavated castles had yet to be decided, both on the evidence of his discoveries, and according to our fundamental principles. The sheltering of the exposed walls against destruction by rain, wind or frost, by means of a protective building, as used in the case of Roman and medieval ruins, could not be considered, if only because of the size of the ruins involved. Apart from the preservation of the masonry itself, the only thing experts could do was to try and protect the battlements *(corona muralis)* and, where it seemed possible, to cover the more valuable and vulnerable finds (such as, for example, a medieval oven or surviving parts of a floor) with a protecting roof. In some rarer cases, where the camber of the arches or the shape of the roofing was known, we experimented with the restoration of the original roofing. Thus the remains of Hungarian castles present the visitor with a picture of preserved ruins, completed only at certain points for the sake of interpretation, or covered at others for protection.[44]

The *Castle of Diósgyőr,* situated in picturesque surroundings near the industrial city of Miskolc was built in the second half of the fourteenth century on the site of an earlier structure which had been surrounded by a more or less circular wall. It is known to have been the favourite residence of the Hungarian King Louis I (the Great). In its second period the castle had four angle towers, of the type that had gained ground in Hungary (probably under the influence of Italian models) during the period when fire arms did not yet influence the construction of bulwarks. In the second half of the fourteenth century the combined functions of fortification and residential palace resulted in the erection of a good many similar fortresses in Hungary (in Tata and Várpalota, for example) with a symmetrical ground plan and walls broken by windows. The Diósgyőr fortress remained in the possession of Louis I till his death; later it was extended by Sigismund and Matthias, but lost its roof in a fire at the beginning of the nineteenth century, after which it suffered steady decay. Three of its four towers could also be reconstructed internally. The fifteenth-century round bastion has been experimentally completed with modern material; it now houses a small museum. The fourth tower and the rest of the remaining fragments of the castle walls are being exhibited as preserved ruins.[45]

The *Castle of Sümeg,* built by the Bishop of Veszprém in the thirteenth century, and developed in the fifteenth, sixteenth and seventeenth centuries, has been restored

XI. Siklós, Castle Chapel: Fresco, 14th to 15th century

in a similar way. It is the largest historical monument of its kind in the vicinity of Lake Balaton and has come down to us with a comparatively large part of its walls still standing. The castle is situated on the peak of a barren hill; its ground plan is irregular in shape with four inner towers. Three of the latter have been roofed in while the rest of the walls has been preserved in their original ruined condition. The gatehouse is now used as an office- and guard-room, the Old Tower houses an exhibition, while the third, the so-called Kövesbástya, is actually destined as an observation tower where a canopy serves for the protection of both the visitors and walls against the weather.[46]

The same dual principle guided the restoration of the *Castle of Nagyvázsony,* also situated in the region of Lake Balaton. Here the quadrangular layout is connected with a fifteenth-century keep which has survived intact. Together with the chapel, which has been roofed in, the keep now serves as an exhibition hall, while the barbican, the living quarters and the fortifications are displayed as conserved ruins.[47]

In connection with Nagyvázsony, it is interesting that this village, situated about sixteen miles from Lake Balaton, and numbering only a few thousand inhabitants, had no tourist traffic at all until the restoration of its castle. Since then it has become a favourite tourist centre on the northern shore of the Lake; it has a riding school—and attracts guests with its historical pageants several times a season. The preservation of the castle was followed by the development of the surrounding area, which resulted in the restoration of a Lutheran church of lesser architectural value, and of a rural dwelling house, as well as by the restoration of the Paulite monastery mentioned earlier, and of a Gothic church. The work in the village will be completed with the reconstruction of the manor house of the Zichy family, a building in neo-Classical style. Nagyvázsony is a good example of how the restoration of a monument can bring in foreign tourists, and how a neglected small community may develop into a favourite excursion centre.

Among the castles preserved in a ruined state, we should mention the *Castle of Várgesztes* which, from the technical point of view, represents a sort of transition, for here we have succeeded in establishing a tourist hotel with the use of the original ground plans and without altering or reconstructing the exterior of the fortress. A combination of the fortress and the stately mansion, Várgesztes was a special type of castle; built in the fourteenth century, its rectangular court is not enclosed on all sides, but a palace wing with Gothic windows joins it at both of its extremities. The excavated fortification walls have been preserved as ruins, but a dining-room and other service rooms of the hotel could be furnished in both wings of the palace. The shape of the original roof could not be detected; it has been replaced by a flat roof concealed behind the ruins, from which a magnificent

XII. Csempeszkopács: Fresco, 17th century

view opens on the wooded peaks of the Vértes Mountains.[48]

The last example brings us to a discussion of the few castles which we are able to put to modern use. First of all, we will consider the *Castle of Buda*. We refer to it at this point for the sake of completeness, but we must refrain from going into details and even from discussing the subject in broad outline. Its history is so rich and the problems of its excavation and restoration so involved that their proper treatment lies beyond the scope of the present volume, and even beyond that of a monograph. It is not accidental, therefore, that in addition to a mass of studies and polemical treatises, whole series of special monographs deal with certain periods of the castle's history, as well as its excavation and reconstruction.

There is hardly another building in Hungary that incorporates so much of the country's cruel history as the Castle of Buda. Built on the site of a prehistoric settlement, it became the permanent residence of the Court, and thus the centre of the country in the second half of the thirteenth century. When the town of Buda turned against the Angevins—the ruling House supported by the Pope—the Court moved to Visegrád and the Castle of Buda lost some of its importance. However, following the economical and political reforms of the middle of the century it again became the permanent royal residence. At the beginning of the fifteenth century the Castle was developed by the Emperor Sigismund who built the so-called New Palace (Friss Palota) which, according to the records of contemporary travellers, was compared to the most famous edifices of the age, such as the Salone of Padova, or the Paris Parliament. Buda was also the major scene of the building activities of King Matthias, during the transition from the Gothic to the Renaissance style, but what is more, it appears to have also been the centre of his creative side as a patron of the arts. The Buda Palace housed his world-famous library, with the manuscripts generally known as Corvinas; the royal bronze-casting workshop—whose products of statues, bronze gates and sepulchral monuments erected in different parts of the country, are only known to us from contemporary records—was probably also situated on the castle premises. The same was probably true of the maiolica workshop which, working at first according to a technique adopted from Italy, turned out paving tiles marked with the emblem of Matthias, even for buildings in such places as Visegrád, Vác and Eger. It also produced tiles with mixed glazing and figural decorations for stoves, as developed by earlier Hungarian craft. Objective archaeological data leaves hardly any doubt that Renaissance pottery, with its new techniques, as well as Renaissance stone carving, started on its way to the North and West of the Continent from Buda. At the beginning of the sixteenth century the Castle was fortified with modern defences, but in 1541 the Turks took it without a shot being fired.

The Turks themselves built hardly anything: instead

they held the Castle at the expense of the existing structure which became severely damaged in the siege liberating Buda in 1686. Practically only a heap of ruins remained of the medieval royal palace, no part of which could be used for the restoration. Following the building operations at the beginning of the eighteenth century—mostly of a military nature—the idea of rebuilding the Castle, and the desire for the revival of the former capital prevailed with increasing force, until the construction of a royal palace was actually started under the reign of Maria Theresa (1740–1780). The project, which was executed with numerous changes of architect, plans and objectives, was completed at the end of the century; it resulted in a block of buildings which was, however, turned over to the University of Nagyszombat then moving to Buda.

It was not without reason that one of the major aims of the 1848–1849 War of Independence was to capture the Castle of Buda; nor was it accidental that after the Austro-Hungarian Compromise of 1867 the idea of erecting a royal palace on Castle Hill was soon brought forward once again. The work was started according to the plans of Miklós Ybl, and completed between 1896–1903 under the direction of Alajos Hauszmann.

An approach involving the excavation and display of the remnants of the medieval and Renaissance palaces and their furnishings was far removed from the contemporary approach, and even from the political trend of the period. The plans provided by Hauszmann were well abreast of his times; he ingeniously developed the Maria Theresian style, and crowned Castle Hill with a complex of buildings which assumed a dominating role in the townscape of Budapest.

The huge building lacked a function not only under the Habsburgs who regarded the Buda Palace as a temporary residence only, but also between the wars, when it only housed a few unimportant offices, as well as the apartment of the Regent. As a last refuge of the encircled German army, it suffered severe damage under the siege for the liberation of the city in 1944–1945.

We cannot at this point dwell upon the vast number of suggestions put forward in connection with the post-war use of the Castle. Suffice it to say that the plans ranged from its preservation in state of ruins in protest against war, to its development into a university centre, or a Hungarian Kremlin. While the question of its utilization was being decided, it was possible to dig up a considerable part of the grounds of the Royal Palace. These excavations, continuing for over ten years, revealed a number of restorable units of architectural interest. Once belonging to the medieval castle and palace, they were the lower floor of the chapel, the southern hall, and the so-called treasury, as well as some ruins suitable for exhibition. The finds unearthed were, however, of considerably greater significance. Gothic and Renaissance fragments, splendid sculptured ornaments, an incredibly large number of objects bearing witness to our early culture, have come to light. The excavations have also clarified most of the construction periods, and provided information on the high artistic standard of the Court in the period from the fourteenth to the sixteenth century.

It was not until after 1957 that the proposal for turning the Royal Palace into a cultural centre housing the National Gallery, the Historical Museum of Budapest, the National (Széchényi) Library, and the Museum of Modern History, was put forward.

The medieval architectural remains, such as the chapel, the southern hall with the barrel-vaulted rooms beneath it, and especially the remains of the fortifications, have been preserved, as far as our principles of restoration allowed, with some interpretative completion. In its exterior the eighteenth-nineteenth century palace now follows the main patterns of the Baroque and neo-Baroque styles, while the development of the interior, especially the ornamentation of the rooms, has been adapted to the new function. Among the almost completely destroyed apartments, the neo-Baroque ornaments of the eighteen-fifties will be restored to the Throne Room. Of the total project, the housing of the Historical Museum of Budapest within the Baroque palace, and the restoration of the adjoining medieval and Renaissance buildings (including their interior and that of the fortifications) are complete, while the restoration work of the palace for cultural purposes is planned for the beginning of the seventies.[49]

The restoration of the *Castle of Gyula* was given high priority in view of the fact the Turkish devastation had left the Great Hungarian Plain extremely poor in historical monuments, especially in medieval ones. The construction of this large, irregularly laid out brick castle began in the fourteenth century, but its present form dates from the end of the fifteenth, and the restoration carried out under the auspices of the National Inspectorate has been based on this later structure. Apart from certain slight pieces of completion, our work has been confined to the exhibition of some of the details unearthed and also to the protection of the substance of the building. At the present time the castle serves as a museum. It is situated in splendid natural surroundings and, together with its restored moat, forms one of the most valuable items of architectural and historical interest in this town which is also famous for its thermal springs.[50]

The restoration of the *Castle of Siklós* is nearing completion. A fortress had stood on this isolated elevation of the country's southern range of hills as early as the second half of the thirteenth century, but its development falls into the Gothic period, or more precisely, into the fourteenth century. The chapel of the fortress has survived in its late fifteenth-century form. With its valuable frescoes and Renaissance details it represents the most beautiful Gothic interior of its kind in Hungary. The Gothic barbican obtained its present form in the first half of the eighteenth century. In the course of recent excavations a bay-window has been found which is without equal in Hungary, not only on account of its form, but also for the richness of its details.[51]

The excavation and restoration of the *Castle of Eger* constitutes, as we have seen, one of our major tasks, and still requires about ten years of work. The fortress played an important role in Hungarian history, for in 1552 István Dobó successfully defended it with a few thousand men against the 100,000 strong Turkish army, thus protecting Upper Northern Hungary (Slovakia) from the invasion. Nevertheless, in 1592 the by then modernized castle fell into the hands of the Turks and was liberated only in 1686. The building was under military control for a long time. The excavation of its casemates and connecting passages was started in the nineteen-thirties, and ten years ago the whole complex was turned into a museum. Up to now it has been possible to restore one of the buildings, or to be more exact, to strip it of its mass of alterations. This is the episcopal palace, which is adorned with a Gothic archway. It is presumed that this part of the complex had been restored using some of the earlier structure in the third quarter of the fifteenth century. From the restoration aspect it presented two technical problems. In the Gothic archway on the ground floor the ninth arch and cross vault from the left have survived in their original form; it was necessary, therefore, to preserve their substance and reinforce their supporting power with the least possible damage to the original details. Of the outer pillars, on the other hand, only the base and a few fragments have been unearthed, thus their restoration called for the use of a different method. The architectural design of the first floor was not fully known to us. Its Gothic openings could be restored, and it was also possible to establish that an open and lighter structure must have run above the archway; however, through lack of information on its components, it has been replaced with a simple wall. The building now houses a museum of local history.[52]

From a historical point of view the *Castle of Kőszeg* in the western Transdanubian region is no less significant, for here, in 1532, Miklós Jurisich was able to hold up the Turkish army for several weeks and thus virtually to save Vienna. The excavation of the fortress and the investigation of its walls have produced important finds.

The original, irregularly laid out fourteenth-century fortress with its four inner towers had been rebuilt in the Renaissance style at the end of the fifteenth and beginning of the sixteenth centuries; later, in the Baroque period, an arcaded open loggia was attached to the main front, opening on to the courtyard. This façade is a rare and interesting example of the transition period between the Gothic and Renaissance styles, for part of the typically Gothic windows, with a mullion and transom each, have Renaissance mouldings, and this trend is further emphasized by the purely Renaissance design of the graffito ornament beside the windows.

The block of buildings which during the nineteenth

century, and even up to the time of restoration, had been used as a store-house, could be restored for cultural purposes. One of the wings now contains a museum, and the other a lecture hall, while there is a coffee-bar on the ground floor.

In view of the cultural functions envisaged, it was possible to adapt the castle to its new use with minimal alterations, consisting mostly of the demolition of nineteenth-century immurations. Among other finds, the demolitions revealed in the hall of the newly built stairway a surviving wall with painted and traceried windows which had originally formed part of the ruined northern wing.[53]

Finally, we have to mention the *Rákóczi Castle at Sárospatak* which had again been given priority for restoration because of its historical significance and outstanding architectural value. The core of this fortress is a huge keep whose date has not been settled: the question is whether the keep had formed part of the development of the royal palace mentioned as early as the second half of the thirteenth century, or whether it was only built in the second half of the fifteenth century. Between 1530 and 1562 the keep was encircled by a wall with contemporary Italian bastions, and a Renaissance-style palace was added to the building by Imre Perényi and his son. At the beginning of the seventeenth century the castle passed into the property of the Dobó family, and later, through the marriage of Zsuzsanna Lórántffy, one of the great supporters of Reformation in Hungary, it became the seat of the Rákóczis. The Transylvanian Prince, György Rákóczi I, carried out important constructions in the middle of the seventeenth century, by which he not only fortified but also improved the building. The alterations resulted in vaulted spaces, among them the reception halls adorned with Kuthaian tiles. Prince Ferenc Rákóczi II, the leader of the war of independence at the beginning of the eighteenth century, had spent his childhood in the Sárospatak Castle and it was from here that, after the failure of his campaigns, he went into voluntary exile. His estates were confiscated, and Sárospatak Castle passed successively into the hands of the Trautsohn, the Bretzenheim, and the Windischgrätz families. The new owners remodelled the building according to nineteenth-century taste. It is a piece of good fortune that they only "restored" the Renaissance Perényi loggia, and that they did not destroy the stone carvings but incorporated them into the residential part of the building. Our restoration work was also greatly facilitated by the fact that in 1883 Viktor Myskovszky documented the situation prior to the latest alterations by technical surveys.

When the Rákóczi Castle of Sárospatak came under public ownership, the protection of the keep was immediately put in hand, as one corner of its structure had been ruined during the systematic destruction of Hungarian castles by the Habsburgs at the beginning of the eighteenth century. In the State Room the original Renaissance wood-carvings have been replaced; this was followed by the restoration of the Perényi loggia and of the later wings of the building. The excavations carried out at the same time around the keep have revealed the underground floor of the tower with a series of multi-branched loop-holes unequalled in Hungary, and yielded a rich store of ceramic fragments. The keep and the later wings of the building have been turned into a museum, and thus, the Castle of the Rákóczis now serves the needs of public education.[54]

The *Castle of Egervár* is also built in the Renaissance style. On the basis of its ground plan and Italian-style angle towers it may be assumed that, together with similar castles in Transylvania and Upper Northern Hungary, it was constructed at the beginning of the sixteenth century. The problems presented by its restoration were mainly related to its situation, since the castle, built on marshland, was supported by stakes which, after the drainage of the waterways involved became exposed to air and deteriorated. Today, the building is used in winter for educational purposes, and in summer for recreation.[55]

COUNTRY PALACES AND MANOR HOUSES

The castles used as residences differ from the big manor houses only in having fortifications. It is evident historically that the building of new manor houses could only begin after the expulsion of the Turks and the defeat of Rákóczi's war of independence, during the economic consolidation of the thin social layer formed by the prosperous classes of the country, that is, in the second half of the eighteenth century, and in the Reform Era of the first third of the nineteenth century. Thus most of our manor houses are built in the late Baroque or neo-Classical style.

Today, the conservation of manor houses is one of our most serious concerns, for the style of living that they had served disappeared between the two world wars. Now the restoration and maintenance of the buildings involved is only possible if they can be put to a suitable use. There are 530 listed country palaces and manor houses in Hungary, for many of which, unfortunately, we have not yet succeeded in finding an appropriate function.[56]

The restoration of the *Palace at Ráckeve* designed in 1702 by J. L. Hildebrandt, the eminent Austrian architect, for Eugène of Savoy have also been commenced. The restoration plans envisage the housing of a museum in the building, and aim at attracting tourists to the locality.[57] The fortified Manor House of the Mágócsy's at *Pácin* has been restored to serve as a school. Its ground plan bears witness to its medieval origin, while the Renaissance graffito ornamentation on the battlements dates from the seventeenth century.[58] The *Mansion at Szigliget*, restored with the use of medieval and Baroque details in the neo-Classical period, and its splendid park, preserved as an arboretum, are today used by the Literary Fund, as a rest-house for writers. The *Ráday Mansion at Pécel*, built between 1722 and 1730, has been turned into a sanatorium for workers on the Hungarian State Railways.[59] Although this function is not ideal for a Baroque castle, we have been able to preserve and suitably exhibit the Baroque mural paintings of the building, including some that have only been revealed during our restoration work. The *Manor House at Noszvaj* has also become famous for its frescoes, part of which had been executed by József Zách on the basis of engravings by E. A. Petitot, a pupil of Soufflot. The pictures were apparently meant to spite Baroque traditions, for they ridicule the antique gods. The mansion is now a rest-house.[60]

As we have said, it is extremely difficult to transform a stately manor house into a hospital without causing damage in its artistic value but the huge parks by which they are surrounded predestine them for this function. It was for this reason that the *Grassalkovich Palace of Hatvan* (1754–1763)—one of the finest examples of Hungarian palace-building under Maria Theresa[61]—has been turned into a hospital, and the neo-Classical *Esterházy Mansion of Csákvár* (designed by the French architect, Charles Moreau, around 1823) into a sanatorium.[62]

The *Episcopal Mansion of Fertőrákos*, dating from the middle of the eighteenth century (its fine frescoes were painted by Caietano di Rosa in 1745) now houses the offices of the Municipal Council.[63] The *Manor House at Nagytétény* (the latter formerly a village, now a district of Budapest) is comparable in its beauty to the *Grassalkovich Palace of Hatvan;* it is one of the finest Hungarian variations of the Baroque country palace. This eighteenth-century building was erected on the foundations of the Roman camp at Campona. Today it serves as a museum. Its rooms are furnished in various styles, so that the visitors may gain a picture of the interior decoration of manor houses and country palaces at different periods. Here, too, mural paintings have come to light as a result of the restoration of the building. They are not by important foreign masters, but they are important nevertheless because they represent the average artistic level of the period. It has been possible to preserve the paintings on the walls where they fit in well with the rest of the museum.[64]

The restoration or—to apply the term used in international literature—reanimation of historical monuments is, as has been seen, chiefly a problem of finding an appropriate new function for the building involved. This may require certain sacrifices but only to the extent that it on no account affects the value of the building as a historical monument. The National Inspectorate therefore always insists on retaining the shape and the original façade of

XIII. Sárospatak: Fresco of the *Sub rosa* chamber, 17th century

the buildings, but of the internal elements it requires only the preservation of those developed with special architectural emphasis (generally the vestibule, main staircase, or state room) or rooms whose walls are adorned with frescoes or stucco. The Inspectorate does not object to the alteration of the rest of the rooms in accordance with the new function of the building, provided of course that such alterations do not affect the façade.

The restoration of the former *Esterházy Palace at Fertőd* presented special problems because of the rich internal development of the building. Miklós Esterházy, surnamed by his contemporaries "the Magnificent" on account of his wealth and patronage of the arts, developed the palace from his hunting seat in Fertőd between 1764–1766, probably making use of the original building but mainly according to his own ideas. His conception was based on the *Schloss of Schönbrunn* in Vienna as a model. The Esterházy Palace—called "the Hungarian Versailles"—is unique in Hungary. Its 126 rooms had made it the largest, and its artistic decoration and furnishing, the richest palace in the country, while the musical traditions associated with it raised it to European fame, for Joseph Haydn had lived in the palace and played music in the opera-house attached to it for over a quarter of a century.

The palace had suffered extremely severe war damage and the retreating troops carried off a great part of its art treasures. After the retreat of the front, it was used as a field hospital, and later as a store-house. In spite of these circumstances we were able to restore the building comparatively rapidly after a suitable new function had been found for it, and although the gilding of the rococo wood-carvings of its state rooms is still incomplete, and we have not been able to replace all the art treasures, nor to restore much of its huge park, yet we managed to complete the essential restoration of the building proper by 1959, the hundred and fiftieth anniversary of Haydn's death.[65]

One wing flanking the vast court of honour now houses the Agricultural Research Institute, the other the Agricultural Training School, while the impressive central block of the palace has been turned into a Haydn Museum. The music of the great Austrian master may be heard in the state room several times a year.

XIV. Sümeg: Fresco by F. A. Maulbertsch. Second half of 18th century

PUBLIC BUILDINGS

The restoration of public buildings was far less problematic, since they had either been built for their present use, or could be adapted by a suitable division of the offices, in accordance with the modern requirements of the preservation of historical monuments.[66] A large number of neo-Classical County Halls were built in the first half of the nineteenth century; most of them still serve as the seats of County Councils. The present seat of the Council of the County of Pest was built by Mátyás Zitterbarth. Its war damages have now been repaired and the building now continues to fulfil its earlier function in its original form. The situation is the same with the Council Halls of the Counties of Tolna and Fejér, and many other Town and County Council buildings. The neo-Gothic Parliament building, designed by Imre Steindl in 1894–1904, and constituting one of the main symbols of the townscape of Budapest, will take several years more to restore. The deterioration of its outer stonework requires the gradual replacement of different parts.

The former large *secondary school for girls at Eger,* notable also for its artistic connotations, now houses the Teachers' Training College, and is thus still used for educational purposes. The front of the block, as well as the internal development of the building planned by Jakab Fellner, as well as its fine mural paintings (the work of Franz Sigrist, Franz Anton Maulbertsch, Johann Lucas Kracker and József Zách) and even part of the stoves also designed by the architect, could be preserved.[67]

The situation is similar in the case of the episcopal palaces of architectural interest. The National Inspectorate has restored the Episcopal Palace of Győr, including its Gothic chapel, as well as the Episcopal Palace of Veszprém, another work of Fellner's. Also restored have been the Episcopal Palace of Pécs, built on medieval foundations but remodelled in the Baroque period, and again in the nineteenth century, and the Episcopal Palace of Szombathely, built by Hefele, the great master of the late Baroque style. (Part of the wing of the last-mentioned building was destroyed during World War II.)

The Vigadó (Municipal Music Hall) of Pest, built by Frigyes Feszl in 1859–1864, is the earliest and also the most lasting architectural work executed in the Hungarian romantic style. Apart from its architectural value, the Vigadó has been a dominant feature of the Pest townscape. The building was extremely severely damaged during the war. After its full restoration, it will again be used as a concert hall and as a gallery for art exhibitions.[68]

The *Palace of the Grand Provost at No.* 2 *Káptalan Street in Pécs* has been restored for public purposes. The restoration revealed that part of the house, mentioned in records as early as the fourteenth century, is medieval. Its façade was adorned by Renaissance windows. The wing attached to the building in the Baroque period is also of considerable architectural interest. The applied arts collection of the Janus Pannonius Museum has been installed in the restored building.[69]

Some of our public buildings of architectural interest were originally designed as museums and still function as such. The Hungarian National Museum, built by Mihály Pollack, between 1837 and 1847, and also severely damaged during the war, now holds the collections of the museum proper and the National (Széchényi) Library. A fine example of Hungarian *art nouveau,* the Museum of Applied Arts (1893–1896) designed by Ödön Lechner, has regained its characteristic coloured glazed tile roof and pyrogranite finials after repairs of the damage suffered during the war and in 1956.[70] It is perhaps necessary to note here that, in our view, the process by which buildings acquire the status of historical monuments is not a matter of the past; it is taking place in our day, too. It would be wrong to confine the protection of buildings to strictly defined periods. Every age produces its own art and architecture according to its own taste and requirements, and it is the duty of the responsible authorities to preserve the best examples of every style. The Museum of Applied Arts is not even our newest historical monument. The *Vas Street School* (built in 1910–1911) and the Martinelli Square business house (built in 1910–1912), both the work of Béla Lajta, one of the great Hungarian pioneers of modern architecture, as well as a number of public buildings, churches and villas, designed by other architects between the wars, have been restored and are now listed as protected historical monuments.[71]

ECCLESIASTICAL BUILDINGS

Churches form the most important section of Hungary's historical monuments, not only numerically, but also from the historical and artistic points of view. Most of them deserve protection both for their architecture and for their internal artistic ornaments and furnishing. The ecclesiastical owners cannot always pay the cost of maintenance, and in such cases the greater part or in some cases the whole of the cost has to be borne by the authorities responsible for the preservation of historical monuments. In some cases the religious community responsible for the maintenance of the ecclesiastical building has ceased to exist or has dwindled to an insignificant number of people. The Turkish buildings, the Greek Orthodox churches of the Serbian minority that had fled the Turks in the Balkans and settled in Hungary in the fifteenth and eighteenth centuries, and the Jewish synagogues are among the items involved. The restoration and maintenance of some highly interesting medieval churches surviving in small villages is almost fully provided for by the National Inspectorate of Historical Monuments.

It is probably best to describe these churches by their stylistic periods, as this will also emphasize the contrasts in methods of restoration.[72]

The style of the Hungarian Romanesque churches shows specific local characteristics. No major Romanesque cathedral has come down to us in its original form; only a few fairly large monasteries preserve the taste of the period, but village churches have survived in large numbers. Their design and proportions and, in a few cases, even their sculptural ornaments and mural paintings make them the lesser gems of our art history. Their restoration has been confined to the excavation of the original ground floor and the remains, if any, of earlier building periods, on the basis of appropriate preliminary archaeological and historical research work.

The recently restored village *church at Egregy* dating back to the second half of the thirteenth century and particularly interesting for the design of its tower, is a church belonging to this category. It is also particularly effectively sited.[73] The *church of Nagybörzsöny* is essentially similar to the one at Egregy; only the carved men's heads on the consoles supporting the cornice of the semi-circular apsis show that it may have been built by a richer community. In addition to the careful restoration of its original form, the modern solution of the interior bears witness to the good taste and restraint of the architect commissioned with the restoration work.[74] The small Romanesque *church of Váraszó* was in ruins, but its excavation enabled us to restore the main cornice and door with its Norman ornaments. The absence of a western tower shows that it belonged to the simpler type of village churches of the period.[75] In its original form, the *Church of Mary Magdalen at Sopronbánfalva* (formerly a small community, now attached to Sopron) may have been similar to the Váraszó church. Its multiangular sanctury and western tower were added only at the beginning of the fifteenth century. In connection with the restoration of the church we have succeeded in bringing to light and restoring some fifteenth-century mural paintings in the nave, and some Romanesque-style murals on the inside of the chancel arch.[76] The *Church of St. Michael at Pápóc,* with a quatrefoil layout, had been likewise built as a village church or funeral chapel. Its split-level structure is regarded as a rare solution for its period, while its red marble door, reminiscent of the style of the chapel in Esztergom Castle, suggests the work of a master of standards.[77]

From among Romanesque churches of the more ambitious type, that of the *Cistercian Abbey at Bélapátfalva,* founded in 1232, heads the list. It is the only Cistercian church in Hungary that has survived.

In the Baroque period the decaying building was plastered over and covered with groined cross vaults. An investigation of its walls threw light on the various architectural periods involved: it appeared that the walls had been erected after the foundation of the monastery, but the supporting system of the vaulting of the church, with its traces of early Gothic style, was built only after the Mongol invasion (1241–1242). Excavations have also clarified the problem of the porch which once stood in front of the western façade and brought to light the remains of the monastery walls, parts of which had crumbled to their very foundations.[78]

The *church at Sopronhorpács* was developed into a two-aisled structure in the Middle Ages. Excavations and the exploration of the walls revealed seven different architectural periods. In the Baroque period, the church was not only vaulted over but its aisle, including its splendid clustered pillars, were immured. For the sake of exhibiting the latter, it was essential to restore the two-aisled structure. The new wall raised on the excavated foundations for this purpose is necessarily up-to-date in formation. The retention of the Baroque interior and especially of the vaulting, did not allow the restoration of the tribune—a characteristic feature of the family-founded Romanesque churches of Hungary; their earlier existence has been indicated, therefore, by the application of simple, contemporary forms.[79]

It was likewise through scientific investigation that the building history of the now *Calvinist church of Karcsa* was elucidated. It was already known that a nave had been attached to what had originally been a round church with a tower, but the reason for this was only clarified by the excavations. The round church with six small semicircular niches forms a group which probably dates from the eleventh century. The church at Karcsa—evidently the parish church of the village—was also of this type. It is presumed that the Order of the Knights of St. John which owned some land in the region, started to build a three-aisled basilica with a transept but, owing to the exhaustion of their material sources, were unable to finish it; instead, they connected the completed nave with the round church they had left standing during the building, and in this form the latter served as a sanctuary. The restoring architect had two problems to cope with. She had to give an idea of the originally planned layout of nave and single aisles, which she achieved with the use of reinforced concrete blades supported by the clustered pillars and by the columns of the chancel arch but serving at the same time as supports for the roofing, and had to provide a substitute for the ungainly ridge turret added to the building on the occasion of its restoration in 1896; this she did by erecting a detached bell tower in a modest modern style.[80]

Among the Romanesque ecclesiastical buildings restored in the past decade, the *provostal church at Felsőörs,* near Lake Balaton, is perhaps the most fortunate example.

The excavations and the associated research work showed that the two-aisled, galleried basilica that has a western tower and a nave terminating in a horseshoe apse, had been built in the first half of the thirteenth century in two periods. The tower, which constituted the first part, may have been meant to stand as a detached structure; the nave with the aisles built with a slightly diverging axis were added later. The piercing of the aisles with low coupled windows is unique in Hungary and, as far as we know, in the whole of Europe, not counting the church of S. Juan de Baños, built several centuries earlier. As a large number of tombs have been unearthed both in the tower and the aisles, it may be assumed that the specially designed aisles had been built as a burial place for the founding family. The details and the vaulting of the square sanctuary bay are Danubian, yet their artistic origin is to be sought in the Italian Cistercian workshops; the fine texture of the walls also points to this source. When the church was restored in the Baroque period, the original Romanesque cornice was put back in place. With the latest restoration the unique harmony of the two styles has been retained. This was the more desirable, as the characteristic popular wood-carvings of the pulpit and high altar—also recently restored—were likewise Baroque in style.[81]

From among the Gothic ecclesiastical buildings several larger ones which represented more intricate problems have been restored. One of these, the *Roman Catholic church at Mátraverebély* was developed from a small Romanesque village church into a large and richly adorned two-aisled basilica, in two Gothic construction periods. In the eighteenth century the church was covered with a Czech-type Baroque surbased vault; and in order to sustain it, the pillars were reinforced with brick. In the course of restoration, it was possible to indicate the place of the Romanesque church in the brick floor and to restore what survived from the two Gothic periods. It would have been wrong to remove the Baroque reinforcement of the pillars and the vaulting; they were only pulled down in the main sanctaury, as there the immured Gothic windows extended beyond the springing line of the Baroque vaulting. Through this modification the Gothic springers and above them parts of the ribs of the cross vaults came to light but the completion of these elements could not unfortunately be considered. Thus the sanctuary got a higher flat wooden roofing which permitted the opening up of the windows and the exhibiting of the remains of the Gothic cross vaults.[82]

The restoration of the *Roman Catholic church at Sárospatak* required even more extensive alterations. The final medieval shape of this large Gothic hall church had been developed through different periods. In the sixteenth century its polygonal sanctuary was demolished for reasons associated with the defence of the castle, while a new vaulting was built in Baroque times.

The excavations have brought surprising results. A Romanesque round church was unearthed close beside the Gothic building; the fine ashlars give much authority to the assumption that it had been built under royal sponsorship in the eleventh century. In the Gothic church, after removing the filling, over three feet deep, used for levelling the ground, the archaeologists struck upon the monumental bases of the Gothic pillars and dozens of tomb-slabs, complete and in fragments, from the sixteenth and seventeenth centuries. Naturally, with the restoration of the late Gothic flooring the internal space was considerably increased. The church is decorated with the artistically extremely interesting Baroque altars and an organ chest purchased on the dissolution of the Carmelite order in Buda. These furnishings have also been partly restored.[83]

The third large Gothic church has been restored is the *Calvinist church of Nyírbátor* built by the Báthorys, one of the richest Hungarian aristocratic families, at the end of the fifteenth century. Originally a Roman Catholic church, it consists of a single huge hall, united by a reticulated vaulting suspended from a barrel vault, which gives the space almost Renaissance proportions. Later, the building was adorned with Renaissance architectural details (south door, coats of arms, sepulchral monuments). The splendid inlaid pew of the Báthorys', an Italian Renaissance work which is now the pride of the Hungarian National Museum, stood once in the choir. Beyond the preservation of the substance of the church, restoration work aimed at the exhibition of the architectural details newly brought to light, such as the Renaissance south door.[84]

The restoration programme of the Inspectorate included several smaller *Gothic churches. St. Stephen's at Nagyvázsony* belongs to this group. It was erected on the site of a Romanesque church in 1481, by the legendary warrior of the Turkish wars, Pál Kinizsi, who owned the local castle and was also the founder of the Paulite monastery. The church, severely damaged in the eighteenth century, was adorned with a new West Tower, altars and a pulpit in a popular Baroque style in 1773. The scope of restoration extended to the two-bayed nave, both having Gothic reticulated vaults, as well as to the Baroque wood-carvings, adding thereby a great deal to the historical interest of the small town.[85]

Sopronbánfalva, the village attached to Sopron, has, in addition to the Romanesque Church of Mary Magdalen mentioned earlier, a second, fairly large *Gothic church* built by the Paulites at the end of the fifteenth century. The building has lost much of its value as a historical monument not only because of the remodelling of its nave in the Baroque period, but also through the fact that, having become a Paulite monastery church at the end of the nineteenth century, its chancel was immured with its space split into two levels by the addition of a floor. The restoration of the chancel and the completion of minor defects in the Gothic vaults did not present any special problem and resulted in an extremely fine spatial effect.[86]

Numerous medieval village churches have come down to us in the north-eastern corner of the country, unvisited by the Turks. This flat region, poor in stone, had developed a special architecture of its own, using glazed bricks for ornamentation. The *Calvinist church of Csenger* belongs to this category, although its dimensions exceed those of a village church. Its restoration included the conservation of a painted wooden ceiling dating from 1745[87]. Painted wooden ceilings for covering the nave became fashionable in Hungary with the Gothic style. Most of the early and Renaissance examples are preserved in museums while Baroque ceilings still usually decorate the churches. This art had a wonderfully rich and unique development in Hungary, in which European forms were transfigured by the imagination of folk art. The last medieval church that has to be mentioned here is the *Roman Catholic church of Nógrádsáp*. It deserves attention not only for the picturesque effect of its exterior mass, but also because during its restoration a Gothic door and windows became exposed as well as a considerable amount of fine fourteenth-century frescoes. All this is further evidence of the fact that medieval culture flourished not only in the towns and castles, but also in the villages of Hungary.[88] We may also include two Gothic monasteries in our list of restored ecclesiastical buildings. It is largely on account of the many wars, the Turkish occupation, and other disasters during Hungarian history, that from the several hundred monasteries known to us from charters, only two have survived, and even these only in part. We have already mentioned the restoration of the Benedictine monastery of Pannonhalma; now we should like to describe that of the chapter-house of the former Franciscan monastery in Sopron.

The monastery building, attached to one of our oldest Gothic churches, once the *Franciscan church of Sopron,* mentioned in records as early as 1280, was remodelled in the Baroque period. On this occasion a storey was added to the former structure, and the extra load bent the pillars of the finely proportioned chapter-house. To avoid their collapse, the slender pillars were enveloped in a thick mantle which naturally spoiled the internal effect. Gradually the hall became a lumber room devoid of character. Restoration work began with the unearthing of its floor. This operation brought to light the remains of an earlier Gothic brick floor with impressed ornaments, destroyed by the subsequent building of crypts. Having released the pillars from the load of the upper store, excavations proceeded to explore the walls and re-establish the original situation. The explorations revealed that originally the hall had been covered with a flat roof, and that the chapel-like, quadrangular sanctuary had belonged to the nave. In about the middle of the fourteenth century—probably on the occasion of the Grand Assembly of the Prebendaries in 1340—it was covered with a vault sustained by two central pillars. Later, at the beginning of the fifteenth century, the Gothic building was completed by adding a side-chapel on both the northern and southern sides. The lavishly carved ornaments of the chapter-house—a unique piece of its kind in Hungary—was to remind the monks assembling there of the seven deadly sins, while the bosses of the cross vault showed the symbol of the purified spirit. The vault and the relief only needed to be cleaned of the layers of lime which formed a deposit on them; only the tracery windows of the chapels required completion. A number of Gothic stone carvings are also exhibited now in the restored chapter-house which has now regained its original effect.[89]

XV. Noszvaj: Fresco, 18th century

The unearthing and restoration of the only medieval synagogue in Hungary started with the renovation of a dwelling house at 11 Új Street in Sopron. The house which had a Baroque façade of slight interest claimed the attention of the unsuspecting specialists when a Gothic cross vault was discovered in one of its rooms. The exploration of the walls soon brought surprising results. It was established that the floor of the first storey was of a later date: originally the building consisted of a lofty, two-bayed Gothic hall, oblong in form. The Gothic door and windows have also been uncovered since. It is known from medieval documents available in unprecedented quantity on Sopron that the building was one of the synagogues of what was once the Jewish quarter of the town. It was sold and turned into a civilian dwelling house in 1526, when the Jews were driven out of the town. Our work on the synagogue aimed essentially at the restoration of its original interior; to this effect the ribs of the destroyed first bay have been replaced on the model of the surviving second one. Research has shown that the Sopron synagogue had been built in the second half of the fourteenth century, and was practically identical in design with its counterpart in Miltenberg. Today the building is used as a museum reminding us of the tragic fate of the Sopron Jews in the Second World War.[90]

Before passing on from medieval to Baroque ecclesiastical buildings, we must deal with the restoration of the historical monuments of the Turkish times. During the 150 years of Turkish rule in Hungary the occupying powers naturally erected their own ecclesiastical and public buildings, characteristic *djamis, mosques* and baths, often making use of existing medieval churches and houses. Most of the Turkish buildings were either destroyed or greatly modified between the eighteenth and nineteenth centuries; those which survive represent the most northerly relics of Islamic art. Therefore special care has been devoted to their restoration.

The *djami* of Ghazi Kasim pasha in the centre of Pécs was built using part of the medieval church of St. Bartholomew's. After the Turks had been driven out of the country, it once again served as a Roman Catholic church. The building was extended between the two world wars, on which occassion the walls of the *djami*, its characteristic stalactite vaults and *mihrab* were uncovered and restored. The original Turkish dome was concealed under another of very poor proportions, built at the beginning of this century. It has been, however, possible to restore the earlier structure, and to cover it with red copper plate.[91] The sixteenth-century *mosque* and *minaret* of Yakovali Hassan, also situated in Pécs, survived as a hospital chapel. Since functional considerations did not bind the restoring architects in this case, the edifice could be restored and exhibited without any addition to the original parts.[92]

Another piece of the Turkish heritage of Pécs is the

XVI. Eger, Lyceum: Fresco by Sigrist, 18th century

turbé of Idris Baba—a sixteenth-century octagonal domed sepulchral building. Its original openings have been uncovered with the tomb and mortal remains of the warrior dervish who had also been honoured as a saint.[93] A further famous place of pilgrimage was Gül Baba's *turbé* in Buda. This sepulchral chapel, similar in ground plan and proportions to the one in Pécs, has also been restored.[94]

In connection with Turkish buildings, we have still to mention two baths in Budapest, not only to give the reader a complete picture of the preservation of historical monuments of Turkish times in Hungary, but also because the centrally domed halls of these baths possess actually the reduced architectural forms of the *djamis*. Tradition has it that Sokoli Mustafa pasha commissioned Sinan pasha, the great architect of Islam, with the building of what is today called *Rudas Baths*. The original form of the bath dates back to sometime after 1566. As most of the Baroque and neo-Classical extensions of the building had been destroyed during World War II, we were able to uncover the original block of the domed bath built of ashlars. The bath has an octagonal basin surrounded by ogival arcades whose pillars sustain the semi-spherical dome. A little more survived of *Király Baths*, built under the name of Mustafa's Baths between 1566–1570. Here, in addition to the dome-covered octagonal basin, two smaller side-chambers, similarly covered by semi-spherical domes, and a passage, also date from the Turkish era. Together with the Turkish exterior and interior of the building, the neo-Classical wings enclosing a columned court have also been restored.[95]

Baroque church architecture—introduced in the country after the expulsion of the Turks—was at its best in the second half of the eighteenth century, especially in the late Classical period of the style, which is also considered as the most characteristic style of Hungarian Baroque art. Most important churches, situated mainly in bigger towns and abundantly adorned with sculpture and painting, date from that period.

The restoration of most of the Budapest churches damaged by World War II has been completed. One of the towers of *Pest City Parish Church* had to be completely rebuilt, while its Gothic chancel, hit by a bomb at a critical static point, required propping. The reparation of the war damages provided an opportunity to put back in their original position the remains of a painted Gothic tabernacle.[96]

From among the restoration carried out in provincial towns we should draw attention to two items. The first, the *Cathedral of Szombathely*, had suffered extremely severe war damage: several hits had reduced its dome to ruins and damaged its nave. The architectural restoration of the cathedral—built by Menyhért Hefele in a restrained late Baroque style between 1791 and 1797—was carried out by the episcopacy within a few years after the end of the war. But the war has caused some irrevocable losses to the Cathedral. It was impossible to save the fresco of the dome, the last work of F. A. Maulbertsch's, and to restore the warm-hued artificial marble facing of the whole interior of the church, which was also destroyed by bombs.[97]

The restoration of another fine example of Hungarian provincial Baroque, the *Minorite Church of Eger,* did not present any special problem. The building deserves mention, however, because of its Italianate stone façade, a feature unique in Hungary.[98]

The Serbian Greek Orthodox churches of Hungary all belong to this period, with the only exception of *Ráckeve Church* whose original structure, dating from the end of the fifteenth century, is the earliest Gothic hall church extant in the country. Later, the northern side of the building was extended by two side-chapels. The architectural restoration of this church has been completed, but the conservation of its heavily touched up Byzantine mural paintings is a problem still awaiting solution. The rest of the Greek Orthodox churches were built in the last third of the eighteenth century. Whole Serbian communities fled the Turks from the Balkans and came to Hungary under the leadership of the patriarch Arsenije Crnojević at the end of the seventeenth century. Most of them settled along the main trade routes and waterways of the country, where the eighteenth-century corn trade was handled. They built at least one church each in Baja, Ráckeve, Pest, Vác, Komárom, Székesfehérvár and Miskolc, but each religious community—seven in number—built one of its own at Szentendre. Very few families profess the Greek Orthodox faith in Hungary today, thus the restoration and possible utilization of these churches devolves upon the State. One at Szentendre, as well as the churches at Baja and Vác, have been purchased to house museums; and a national collection of the treasures of Greek Orthodox ecclesiastical art has been assembled in the episcopal palace of Szentendre. A more difficult task than the restoration of the exterior of our Greek Orthodox churches is presented by the restoration of the frescoes, and especially of the extremely rich and fine wall furnishings and icons adorning their interior.[99]

DWELLING HOUSES

Hungarian statistics on graded buildings are headed by dwelling houses which before World War II were believed to date from the eighteenth and nineteenth centuries. On examining their stripped façades and interiors after the damages of 1945, it was found, however, that a great many of the Baroque-style houses had made use of existing medieval buildings. In this connection a single example will tell more than anything else. Before the war, there was a sole architectural monument registered as medieval in part in the whole Castle district of Buda. It was a dwelling house with a cornice on the façade supported by small arcades, and with a couple of *sedilia* and a Gothic vaulted room. As a result of post-war restoration work 84 more or less important Gothic details are known in the 145 dwelling houses listed as historical monuments in the same district today. The same is true for Sopron. It was never expected, however, that Gothic details would emerge on dwelling houses in other provincial cities and towns. When at Vác the present building of the first Hungarian Institute for the Deaf and Dumb was restored to suit it to its special function, its walls were found to have constituted the medieval episcopal palace. One of the medieval canons' houses at Pécs has been mentioned before. At Kőszeg several dwelling houses show traces of medieval origin, while at Székesfehérvár a first-floor Gothic window has been found, besides a number of *sedilia* under different doorways. At Gyöngyös it has been possible to restore a cross-vaulted Gothic hall, probably the medieval town hall, while at Ráckeve the restoration of a Gothic dwelling house is in progress. Under these circumstances it is only natural that damaged houses are as a rule also investigated above their ground levels. Thus the wall exploration techniques of the Hungarian specialists have been developed by the experience gained on dwelling houses. In order to present a survey of this large-scale restoration of damaged dwelling houses, our observations have to be grouped under three heads: the exhibition of the results of explorations; the bringing of the restored buildings up to date and utility; the problem of shop-windows, especially in the case of nineteenth-century houses.[100]

In our view, the exhibition of the results of explorations associated with the restoration of the building in question is a creative process involving architectural problems. The architect in charge of the restoration must carefully distinguish scholarly data which are of theoretical interest and properly belong to the documentation pertaining to the building, from other details which deserve exhibition in any form. With the latter choice, and especially with façades, he must take care to retain the architectural unity of the building. No doubt our architects readily display on Baroque or even on later façades the Gothic details they are able to uncover since the medieval fragments, plastering or mural paintings emerging on house after house may combine to give the passing spectator the impression of a once Gothic town. Experiments in this direction must not, however, result in the disintegration of the architectural unity of the buildings or façades involved.

We may cite as an example the two-storied building at *31, Úri Street* which is our only proof that such large dwelling houses had actually existed in medieval Buda. The essential features of the medieval façade could be restored by modelling the new openings on the measurements of the existing Gothic windows on the second floor. Most of the Gothic details of *36, Úri Street* had perished, only the *sediliae* under the doorway have come down to us. Even so, the displaying of these scarce medieval details has not broken up the unity of the façade of this building. The courtyard and doorway of the neo-Classical house at *2, Országház Street* preserved details of interest unique even in Buda. The Gothic arcades of the yard give an idea of the scope of the inner architecture, and the neo-Classical loggia on the first floor fits in well with the Gothic details. A fine example of stylistical co-existence is supplied by *32, Úri Street*. Except for its doorway, this house had been completely destroyed. The modern building which replaced it incorporates the original doorway lavishly adorned with doors and *sediliae;* even the fact that the Gothic barrel vault of one of the passages of the courtyard passes into Baroque at one end, and the passage leads into a yard of modern design, does not seem to spoil the overall effect.

In the Middle Ages, and even in the Baroque period, the civilian population of Buda maintained farms and particularly vineyards, besides pursuing their industrial and trade activities. This dual occupation explains their use of broad and high doorways and spacious courtyards, unusual in medieval towns elsewhere. Cleared of their outhouses, the yards have been developed into delightful small gardens. It is probably also the dual occupation of the inhabitants which accounts for the fact that the doorways are provided with rows of blind tracery-ornamented late Gothic *sediliae*. The latter, together with the arcaded entrances to the courtyards, and the broad façades with the ridge of the roofs stretching parallel with the street, from a close relationship between the medieval dwelling houses of Buda and their southern counterparts.[101]

Most of the listed dwelling houses in Hungary are unsuited to offer the amenities of modern flats, and the familiar process of buildings in residential sections of architectural or historic interest deteriorating with the gradual changing of their occupants took place in Hungary too. This situation can only be improved by complete modernization which will be the more necessary as most of the ceilings in these houses need replacing. Dwelling houses of architectural interest can only be preserved for the generations to come if the flats in them meet the requirements of modern living. The interior of these buildings and the axis of their windows call for the planning of rooms larger in area and cubic capacity than is usual in modern homes; thus, from the housing point of view, this architectural solution involves a certain loss in the potential number of flats. Rooms of architectural interest covered by vaults or—as we have seen in Sopron—by painted or carved ceilings must naturally be retained as complete units, unaffected by the restoration or modernization required. This principle has been observed in the restoration of a good many houses in Buda and Sopron, where valuable interior mural paintings and carved details have been uncovered (e.g. *32, Szent György Street* and *10, Új Street, Sopron)*. The details thus displayed have been made accessible to visitors by the restorers. With the modernization of listed dwelling houses architects often avail themselves of the advantages afforded by split-level flats and built-in furniture. By way of example, the solution applied with the restoration of the early Baroque loggia with Tuscan columns inside *9, Templom Street in Sopron*, and in *11, Chernel Street in Kőszeg*, may be mentioned.

Problems of a different kind are offered by houses built in the neo-Classical period. The ground floor of nineteenth-century buildings was usually occupied by shops which, as competition increased during the twentieth century, required larger and larger windows. This shop-front rivalry ruined the ground-floor architecture of the buildings, practically splitting their façades into two. The abolishment of this disturbing effect and the re-establishment of architectonic order, with, where possible, the restoration of the original openings of the façade, were considered as a problem of primary importance. Starting from the principle that, where buildings of Category I are involved, the elements of the original architecture should in some cases be allowed to show up, the restorers have reduced the shop windows to their original size. With buildings belonging to Categories II and III the Inspectorate is in favour of creating architectural order by applying a uniform solution. In this connection great care is taken not to impoverish the aspect of urban shopping streets by reducing the shop windows to their original, generally smaller size. Especially good results have been achieved on the basis of these considerations in two streets of major importance.

The Budapest Nagykörút (Great Boulevard), running in a semi-circle away from and back to the Danube, had only been built within a few decades in the historical, predominantly neo-Renaissance style prevailing at the end of the nineteenth century. As a result of the restoration campaign started on the basis of unified principles after 1957, most of the shop windows were replaced within their original architectonic frame. A similarly successful experiment has been completed at Pécs, where Kossuth Lajos Street has been developed into a shopping centre, closed to traffic. In addition to remodelling the shop windows of historical monuments, houses of lesser architectural importance were also provided with new shop-fronts, designed to give each building an integral character.[102]

RURAL AND INDUSTRIAL BUILDINGS

The monuments of these two widely differing branches of architecture came under the same heading, at the end of our description, because we are having to cope with difficulties of a similar sort in their restoration. The results we can show up lag behind the urgency of preserving the rapidly deteriorating items involved. With both groups of buildings the rapid decay is due to the fact that they are no longer suited for their functions in modern life.

With regard to industrial architecture no detailed explanation is needed; buildings reflecting the country's earlier manufacturing activity can only be preserved as factories. This group includes the wind- and water-mills which in the Middle Ages played an important part in most branches of industry. According to an estimate dating from the end of the past century, there had been more than ten thousand mills operating on the waters of Hungary. Their power was used for various purposes besides milling and grinding (e. g. fulling). Most of these mills disappeared in the first half of the present century. However, some of the numerous water-mills erected in Tata in connection with the development of the water supply in the eighteenth century are still being operated without any change in the interior details, with the use of electric power. In *Túristvándi,* it was possible to restore a highly picturesque three-wheeled *water-mill,*[103] while at Ráckeve the last water-mill on the Danube has been preserved and will now be placed in the national open-air museum of peasant architecture.[104]

In the Great Hungarian Plain the wind-mills were a characteristic feature of the landscape. Today only about a dozen remain; they are under protection and some of them have already been restored (Karcag, Szeghalom, Kiskunhalas and Szentes).[105] From other branches of industry, a blue-dyeing workshop (complete with equipment) has been preserved in Pápa, where it is displayed as a museum; the same applies to a *dye-house at Szendrő;* and in Budapest the foundry hall of the first building of the Ganz factory, erected around 1840, has been turned into a metallurgical museum. The ancestor of the *Diósgyőr Iron Works,* the foundry built in the picturesque Garadna valley around 1820—a structure of considerable architectural interest—likewise belongs to the earliest preserved metallurgical relics in Hungary. A few village smithies with their original equipment and implements are similarly displayed as museums.

A number of railway buildings are also listed among industrial relics, and some bridges are included in the same category, above all the third symbol of the capital—the *Lánchíd (Chain Bridge)* designed and built by W. T. Clark between 1839 and 1849. A few of the lesser bridges, built in the Baroque and neo-Classical style, like the one spanning the Gombás brook at Vác, with its fine statues, are still in use.

The preservation of historical monuments of strictly ethnographic character presents a similar problem, insofar as the houses in question no longer meet the requirements of the villagers. Better earning prospect provided by the socialist agricultural system as well industrial boom which recruited its man-power chiefly from the country, caused a sudden and radical change in village architecture. However, the change in the appearance of villages as a result of this swing is not as felicitous as it might be. A very high percentage of the dwelling houses built in Hungary at present are in the villages and this naturally affects the fate of village buildings of architectural interest. The owners refuse to maintain obsolete houses which, with their small windows and out-of-date design, fail to satisfy even their basic sanitary requirements. It is the more difficult to take a strong line against this attitude, as the improvement of the social conditions of the villagers is one of the country's most important tasks. The situation is the same with the last relics of peasant farming (barns, sties, press-houses, cellars, etc.) which with the development of large-scale collective farming have completely lost their role. Owing to these circumstances, official protection—which proved satisfactory in towns—cannot be effectually applied for the preservation of buildings of ethnographic interest. Yet the buildings involved are unequalled relics of the creative power of a nation. Among them some highly picturesque items may be found, displaying the masterful use of local building materials, while their inner design, together with the outhouses, provide an excellent picture of the way of life of the Hungarian peasant.[106]

In view of these difficulties, two ways have been found eligible for the preservation of rural architecture: the most important items, especially those forming a whole complex in the tourist centres mentioned earlier, are generally restored on the spot to suit a new function; others are transferred to open-air ethnographic museums. The building of a national open-air museum at Szentendre, and of regional ones in various provincial towns (Zalaegerszeg, Szombathely, Pécs), is in progress.

Successful experiments have been made for the local protection of complexes of architectural interest in the Balaton region. At Tihany the monuments of the building activities of the cottars and fishermen once in the service of the abbey are intended for protection. Their houses—generally built of locally produced stone, and covered with reed thatching—are now either used as ethnographic museums, e. g. a farmer's house with the adjacent fishermen's Guild Hall, or are given a new function, like the two peasant houses turned into restaurants, or the buildings used for the sale of tourist wares.[107] Similar complexes may come into consideration for protection in other villages around Lake Balaton, at Hollókő in the North, the region of Lake Fertő, near the western border where whole streets of fine arcaded houses still exist, and in the Őrség, in the County of Vas, where a so-called enclosed house and a nearby farm building, the latter the only surviving two-storied timber outhouse in Hungary, have been restored.[108]

Further examples of buildings preserved by giving them a new function are the arcaded house at Balatonszentgyörgy, now used as a tourist shop, and the characteristic thatched house at Vitka which serves as a doctor's surgery.[109] At Tiszacsécse, situated in the same region, the birthplace of Zsigmond Móricz, the great novelist, functions as a memorial museum.[110] At Badacsony, the same role has been given to the house which was the home at the beginning of the nineteenth century of Róza Szegedi, wife of the poet Sándor Kisfaludy. The three-storied Baroque building, provided with a bulging balcony, rises on the slope of an extinct basalt volcano, where viticulture has been flourishing since Roman times. It is, both in whole and in part, a fine gem of architecture well suited to the landscape.[111] From the architectural point of view the building is closely related to the Nemesvámos village inn which, having been restored, now fulfils its original function, and is much frequented by tourists.[112] The Tarányi press-house at Szentgyörgyhegy similarly serves as a restaurant. The latter is remarkable, not only for its exceptionally beautiful neighbourhood, bordered by the volcano cones flanking that part of Lake Balaton, but also for the statues adorning the Baroque-lined gable of the storey above the two-aisled cellar.[113]

A special group of rural architectural relics is that of wooden *belfries*. A particularly rich stock of these beautifully shaped architectural masterpieces have survived in the Counties of Szabolcs-Szatmár (Northeast) and Zala (Southwest). The two types current in these regions differ from each other to a certain extent, as the north-eastern group is more closely related to the Upper Hungarian, and the south-western to the Slovenian and Styrian belfries. The most beautiful ones that were in danger of deterioration have already been preserved. From the north-eastern group a turreted belfry built in 1691 in Vámosatya has been restored, and another of similar design in Zsurk, as well as a wooden tower in Gemzse. From the south-western Zala group the Pankasz belfry dating back to 1730 is remarkable.[114]

STATUES AND MURAL PAINTINGS

In the present book in discussing architectural restoration, references have been often made to the restoration of works of art found in or on the buildings. It has also been noted that their restoration is based on the same principles as are applied to architectural objects. With the restoration of works of art it is perhaps even more important that the original parts should by displayed without any attempt at completion. Where their presentation makes completion inevitable, the new parts are added in a different colour or form (e. g. marked with lines) or at a different depth.

Among the sculptures that have been restored the medieval stone carvings should be mentioned first. The main principle here is that deteriorated details found in their original position (e. g. window and door frames) should not be replaced; where completion or replacement is inevitable, we use the locally available breakstone with cement, or natural stone, in a somewhat rougher dressing for the sake of easier distinction between the original and new parts. The case is different with another very important group which includes larger sculptural works. The conceptual foundations of their reconstruction are evident from what has already been said; their practical realization required the team-work of an excellent sculptor-restorer and his colleagues. Their method can be best illustrated by an account of the reconstruction of the Visegrád fountains and the Siklós bay-window.[115]

It has been mentioned that the monuments of medieval art in Hungary have not only to be excavated, but also assembled and reconstructed from fragments. The refined methods of modern archaeology are able to provide the material and observations necessary for this purpose. It was by such means that on the site of the Royal Palace in Visegrád, from the base of a buttress and the Renaissance fountain and from the parapet of the court of honour, several hundred pieces of the Angevin well have been retrieved. The fragments of a red marble fountain built in 1473, with the basin mounted on carved lions and covered with a canopy-shaped top, were discovered in the rubble at the uppermost level of the ruins of the Royal Palace. Moreover, as a result of our excavations on this spot and of the exploration of the neighbouring walls it was also possible to reconstruct the ancestor of this object, a wall fountain, similarly provided with a canopy, but adorned with the coat of arms of Louis I (the Great) (1342–1382). Sufficient details of each of the three fountains have been unearthed to enable their correct reconstruction beyond doubt. Ernő Szakál and his colleagues not only assembled the broken pieces by their fractures, and carefully observed and examined the smallest details, but were also able to discover and display in all three cases the constructional principles their medieval ancestors had employed.

The first fountain has been copied in red marble for exhibition on its original site, while the original pieces have been transferred to a museum. All parts whose form

Visegrád, Royal Palace: Plan for the restoration of the Angevin well-house

Visegrád, Royal Palace: Plan for the restoration of the Lions' Fountain

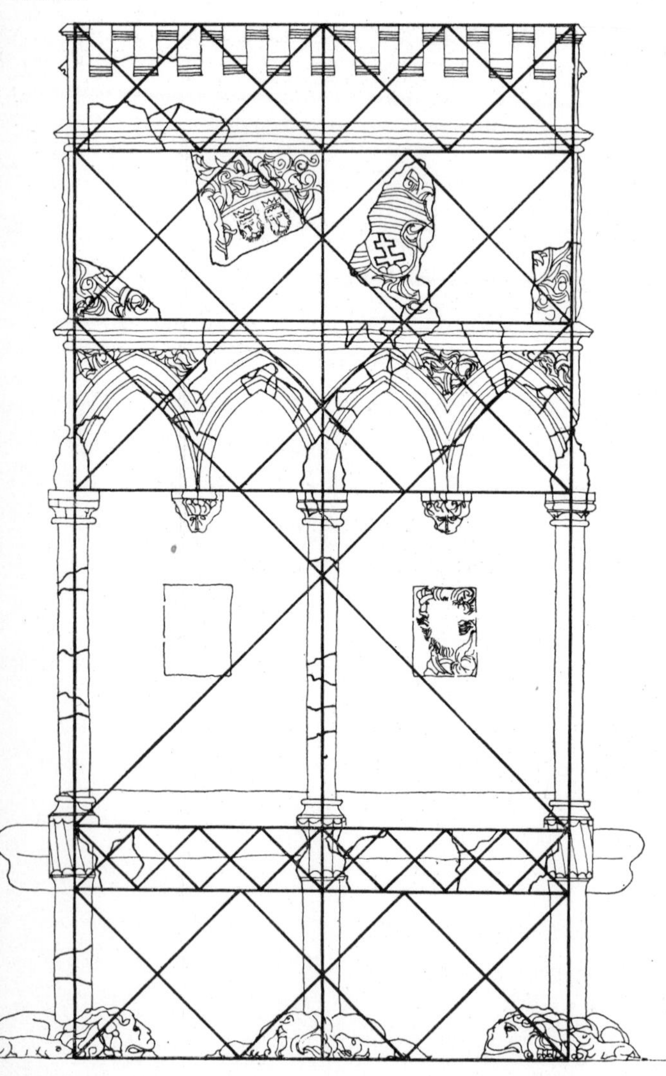

could not be established with certainty on the basis of the original fragments have been left roughly hewn out on the copy (e. g. some of the coats of arms visible on the front). The two other fountains have been reconstructed with the use of the original pieces as it was possible to ensure their protection in doors, in museums. The reconstructions, executed in easily distinguishable concrete, are in harmony with the general appearance of the fountains. The same method was used for the reconstruction of the Siklós bay-window, now back in its original position.[116]

Naturally the activity of our experts on sculptural restoration is not confined to the restoration and conservation of medieval sculptural work; a considerable number of Baroque statues in public squares also require their attention. From the latter group we would mention the statue of St. Michael (1764) and a tabernacle with the Ark of the Covenant, a very unusual sculptural work in Győr (1729), the Trinity column at Vác (1750–1755) and at Veszprém (1750) and from the numerous statues of St. John of Nepomuk, the one restored at Mosonmagyaróvár (1749).

The fragmental condition of the sculptures and carved stone ornaments has made it necessary to provide for their safeguarding in special museums.[117] The first lapidarium set up in 1938 in the building bordering the conserved ruins of the Székesfehérvár Basilica, was arranged by the present writer. In addition to the few foundation

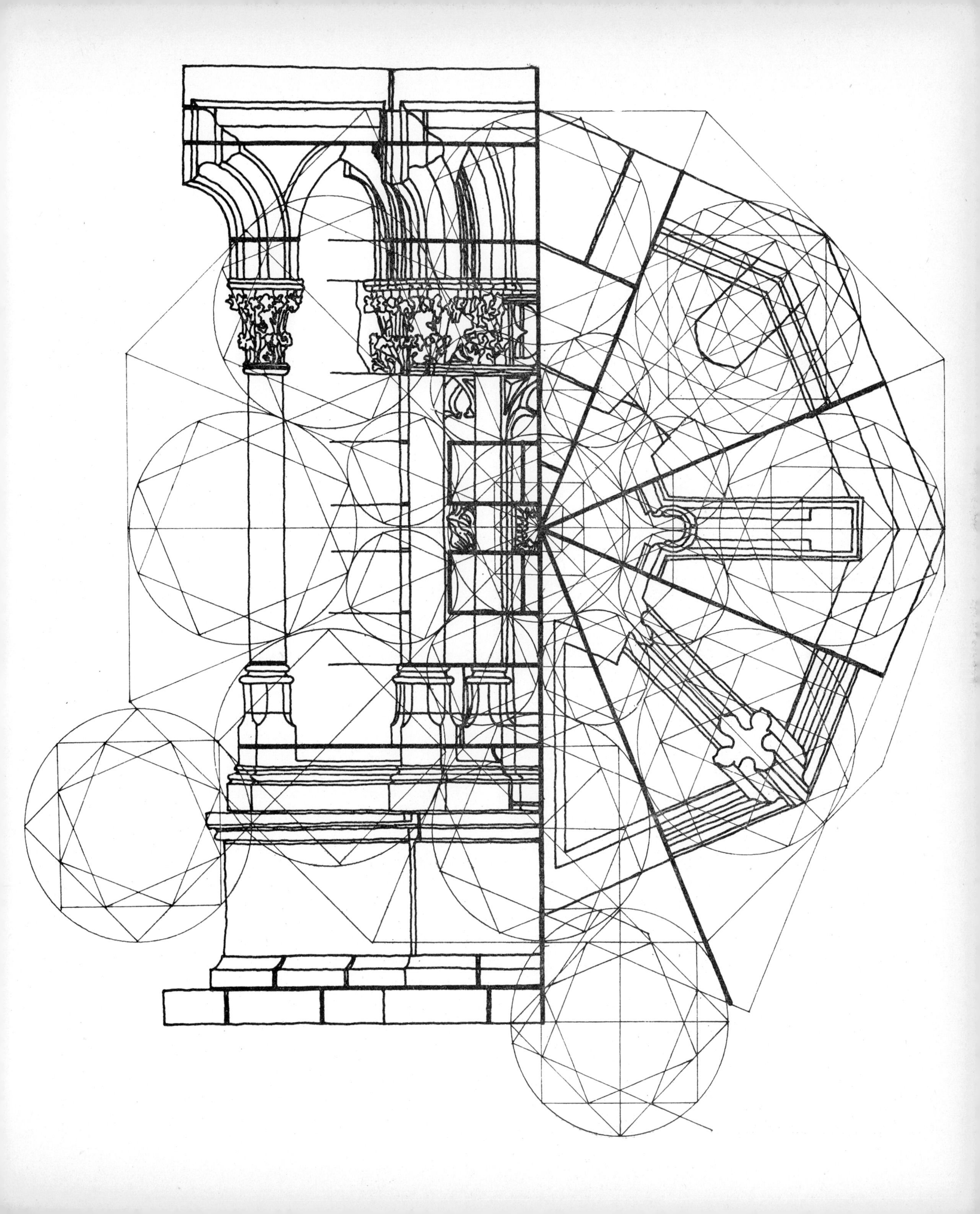

walls remaining on the location, a large number of fragments deriving from Romanesque and Gothic sculptural decorations, as well as St. Stephen's coffin carved from a Roman sarcophagus,[118] and fragments of the funeral chapel and tomb of Louis the Great and other red marble sepulchral monuments, provide at least some idea of the one-time beauty and artistic ornaments of the ancient basilica. The same considerations have prompted the establishment of special Romanesque, Renaissance and Gothic *lapidariums* on the site of the Esztergom excavations, to house the carvings which could not be displayed *in situ*. The arrangement of the material which has accumulated since and is estimated at several thousand items, is in progress. The *lapidarium* of Pécs was founded in 1953; it contains more than 700 pieces removed from the Cathedral over half a century ago, and inadequately stored since then. Part of the material has been restored by completion for the sake of exhibition, while in the exhibition of the rest, we endeavoured to give an idea of their original role.[119] The same procedure was adopted with the exhibition of the stone carvings removed from the Church of Ják to the Szombathely Museum in connection with the restoration of the church in 1956. Our presentation of the severely damaged original parts of the main doorway, and in particular of the erroneously substituted tympanum relief, is especially significant from the historical point of view.

The preservation of wood-carvings involves entirely different, primarily technological problems. Medieval sculptures and ornaments in wood seldom belong integrally to architectural monuments. The exceptions include St. Michael's statue in Sopron, and a Madonna in Ják. Thus our material consists mainly of Baroque, and an insignificant stock of neo-Classical church furnishings. The condition of these sculptures and carvings is, however, rather disquieting, since up to the past decade practically nothing had been done for their preservation. As the churches contain a large number of altars and pulpits of the highest standard, their preservation demands well-equipped and well-staffed specialized workshops. The restoration section of the National Inspectorate of Monuments, and the Enterprise for Works of Art, also active in the restoration of wood sculpture, consider the conservation of the wooden material of these works of art as their primary task. Besides that, their work aims at bringing out the original surfaces and colours from under later coasts of paint and, to a lesser degree, at the replacement of missing details.

One of the earliest undertakings in this field in Hungary was the restoration of the so-called *Krucsay Altar of the Minorite church in Nyírbátor*. Built (together with a number of other surviving altars) in the Eperjes workshop around 1730, this altar is a product of the late sculptural art of Upper Hungary, which, however, carried over the traditions of Gothic naturalism and Renaissance altar-building into the Baroque expressionist style.[120] In current practice the architectural restoration of the churches is combined with the conservation of their wood-carvings, as for example in the case of the Baroque altar of the *Berhida Gothic church*, the altar and pulpit of *St. Stephen's* in *Nagyvázsony*, the *provostal church in Felsőörs*, and the *Calvinist church in Sárospatak*.[121]

In the case of the restoration of mural paintings the Inspectorate relies less on its own workshop than on the cooperation of restorers active within the framework of the Arts Fund. The distribution of the material according to age and quality is far from even: medieval frescoes are rare (most of them date from the fourteenth and fifteenth centuries); large-size Baroque murals mainly by Austrian masters of the first rank are more common. With medieval frescoes we usually insist on remaining within the bounds of conservation, while with eighteenth- and nineteenth-century works we permit distinguishable completions, after the pictures have been repaired and cleaned.

Besides the medieval mural paintings discussed in connection with the restoration of the churches at Feldebrő, Sopronbánfalva, Velemér and Nógrádsáp, special mention should be made here of the frescoes in the chapel of the Castle of Siklós, as after an attempt at their conservation *in situ* had failed, the restorers had to resort to removing them for treatment. As the work involved the conservation of frescoes in different niches, with the pictures extending to three walls each, the team in question had to cope with special technical problems, all the more as in two of the niches the frescoes were to be remounted in their original position after appropriate air-insulation, encased in more or less movable frames.[122]

Reviewing the Baroque mural paintings, we may start our account with two items of special interest. In one of the halls of the *Esterházy Palace at Fertőd* a mural *chinoiserie*, unique in Hungary, has been discovered under a decayed wooden wainscot. It is presumed that it had adorned the wall of the original Fertőd shooting lodge. The second is the murals dating back to 1657, found in the small *Roman Catholic church in Csempeszkopács*. The paintings, which cover practically the whole of the church interior, reflect the naive charm of folk tales and are partly reminiscent of the works of textile and decorative arts of the period.

The most outstanding Baroque frescoes that have been restored are the compositions by Maulbertsch in the *Carmelite church of Székesfehérvár* and the *Roman Catholic church of Sümeg*.[123] By Hungarian standards, both are large-size frescoes. The one in Sümeg is the most fascinating piece of painting among the early works of this "Austrian Tiepolo". Both frescoes required repairing, cleaning and some slight touching up, owing to the damage they had suffered by leaks during the war.

*

In presenting this survey of the most important restoration work carried out in Hungary in the past decade, the author attempted to present the main pursuits of restoration experts and the National Inspectorate, and to illustrate the methods they employ in the preservation of the heavily depleted artistic heritage of the country. He also tried to point out the importance of the basic conditions which most favour the protection of the treasure of cultural history and its introduction in the international current of tourism in a country. These basic conditions are an up-to-date Monuments Act and an appropriate national organization; the application to special national circumstances of the principles and techniques recommended by international agreements; a due consideration of the respective recommendations of UNESCO; and an active participation in the work of ICOMOS. The protection of historical monuments leads to a fuller appreciation of history, both national and universal, and of man's creative genius. In this spirit, this country wishes to contribute to the great international collaboration whose ultimate goal are friendship among nations and peace in the world.

Notes

1. By the protection of historical monuments we understand the conscious preservation of relics of artistic or historic interest: thus we have omitted from our present study allusions to measures and activities which had aimed at the restoration of deteriorated buildings for purely utilitarian purposes. (E.g. the 1091 resolution passed by the Szabolcs Council of King Ladislas concerning the restoration of damaged churches; the order issued by King Sigismund in 1405 for the restoration of the houses of Visegrád; the diploma issued by Louis II in 1526, prohibiting the demolition of a house in the main square of Sopron, lest it should cause a break in the enclosure of the square, etc., etc.) Research work and restoration carried out in recent years have shown that efforts comparable to the protection of historical monuments had already been exerted in the Baroque period. Thus, for the restoration of the Gothic vaulting of the Farkas Street Calvinist church in Kolozsvár (Cluj, Romania), in the middle of the seventeenth century Prince György Rákóczi I invited stone carvers with a special knowledge of Gothic vaults from Kurland. Although in Pannonhalma the eighteenth-century restoration of the door leading to the crypt of the Abbey and of the so-called *Porta Speciosa* shows signs of misinterpretation, the work had evidently been carried out with the intention of following the forms characteristic of the Romanesque style. With the restoration of the provostal church of Felsőörs, also performed in the Baroque period, the stones of the main cornice supported by small arcades regained their original role. Finally, according to one of the unexecuted plans for the reconstruction of the Chapter Hall in Pécs, the coupled windows of the Romanesque hall were to be integrated with the homogeneous Baroque façade of the building. These examples from the Baroque period will, no doubt, increase in number, and supply further valuable data on the antecedents of present-day preservation of historical monuments in the years to come.

In another connection we could mention here the eighteenth-century archaeological explorations for Roman relics. Excavations were performed by István Schönwisner at Szombathely and Óbuda (Aquincum). The ruins unearthed by Schönwisner were also preserved by him, according to the primitive methods of the day.

There is no comprehensive work on the preservation of historical monuments in Hungary available in any foreign language. A good summary in Hungarian, with a short French abstract is László Gerő's *Építészeti műemlékek feltárása, helyreállítása és védelme* [The Excavation, Restoration and Protection of Historical Monuments of Architectural Interest in Hungary]. Budapest, 1958.

2. Ipolyi, Arnold: *A magyar műtörténeti emlékek tanulmánya* [A Study of the Relics of Hungarian History of Art]. Budapest, 1878.

3. Gerő, László: "Hunyadi János vajdahunyadi vára" [The Vajdahunyad Castle of János Hunyadi]. *Műemlékvédelem* (1957), pp. 81–92; with short abstract in French.

4. Levárdy, Ferenc: "Les monuments d'architecture médiévale à Pannonhalma." *Acta Historiae Artium* VIII (1962), pp. 3–44. The more recent excavation was carried out by Katalin H. Gyürky, the exploration of the walls by András Gergelyffy; the restoration was by János Sedlmayr. The restoration of the *Porta Speciosa* is the work of the sculptor-restorers Ernő Szakál and Imre Kőfalvi. Cf. Katalin H. Gyürky—András Gergelyffy—Imre Kőfalvi—János Sedlmayr: "A pannonhalmi kerengő és kolostorudvar helyreállítása"

[The Restoration of the Pannonhalma Cloisters] *Arrabona* V (1963), pp. 121–199; with abstract in French.

5. Lux, Koloman: "Die Burg Visegrád." *Der Burgwart* 39 (1938), pp. 74–85. The first designs for the restoration of Solomon's Tower were made by József Szanyi, the definitive plans by János Sedlmayr. Archaeologist: Miklós Héjj. Szanyi József: "A visegrádi alsóvár" [The Lower Castle of Visegrád]. *Műemlékvédelem* (1959), pp. 11–21; with abstract in French. Sedlmayr, János: "A visegrádi lakótorony helyreállítása" [The Restoration of the Lower Fortress of Visegrád]. *Műemlékvédelem* (1966), pp. 17–27; with abstract in French.

6. Entz, Géza: *L'Église de la Vierge dite église Matthias à Buda et le Bastion des Pêcheurs*. Budapest, 1965. Published also in German and English. The restoration carried out after World War II was designed by László Borsos, the restoration of the relief is the work of Ernő Szakál.

7. Marosi, Ernő: "Beiträge zur Baugeschichte der St. Elisabeth Pfarrkirche von Kassa". *Acta Historiae Artium* X (1964), pp. 229–245.

8. Hajós, Géza: "Die Erneuerung und der Neubau der mittelalterlichen Kathedrale von Pécs im 18. und 19. Jahrhundert". *Österreichische Zeitschrift für Kunst und Denkmalpflege* XXI (1967), pp. 179–185. József Hampel, one of the outstanding archaeologists of his time wrote about the cathedral in the *Archaeologiai Értesítő* 1891, p. 289 . edited by himself, as follows: "...this most remarkable historical monument to our country, dating back to the reign of the Árpád Age, has risen from the ashes, more magnificent than ever", while Béla Czobor, official of the National Commission of Historical Monuments declared: "It is with great pleasure that today we render homage to Schmidt's work of genius... which occupies a prominent place in the history of the restoration of historical monuments." "A pécsi székesegyház restaurációja" [The Restoration of the Pécs Cathedral]. I–VI. parts. *Egyházművészeti lap* (1882), p. 174.

9. Dercsényi, Dezső: "Zur siebenhundertjährigen Feier der Kirche von Ják". *Acta Historiae Artium* IV (1957), pp. 173–202.

10. Forster, Gyula: *A műemlékek védelme a magyar és a külföldi törvényhozásban* [Legislative Protection of Historical Monuments in Hungary and Abroad]. (1906), pp. 219–222.

11. *Magyarország Műemléki Topográfiája*, I. Pest megye műemlékei [Topographical List of Hungarian Monuments]. Vol. I. The Historical Monuments of the County of Pest, Budapest, 1957, pp. 481–496.

12. Entz, Géza : *A gyulafehérvári székesegyház* [The Cathedral of Gyulafehérvár]. Budapest, 1958, with abstract in German.

13. Barcza, Géza: "Műemlékvédelem a magyar Tanácsköztársaság idején" [Preservation of Historical Monuments under the Hungarian Republic of Councils]. *Építés- és Közlekedéstudományi Közlemények* VII (1964), pp. 443–466; with abstract in German.

14. Dercsényi Dezső: *The Royal Palace of Esztergom*. Budapest, 1966. Published also in German and French.

15. Excavation and conservation by Kálmán Lux; the galleries housing the lapidarium around the ruins designed by Géza Lux. Dercsényi, Dezső: *A székesfehérvári királyi bazilika* [The Royal

Basilica of Székesfehérvár]. Budapest, 1943. A short survey, Dercsényi, Dezső: "Székesfehérvár, St. Stephen's City." *The Hungarian Quarterly* IV (1938), pp. 87–96. Dercsényi, Désiré: "Alba Regia." *Nouvelle Revue de Hongrie* (1940), pp. 124–130. Entz, Géza—Szakál, Ernő: "La Reconstitution du Sarcophage du roi Étienne." *Acta Historiae Artium* X (1964), pp. 215–228.

16. Paulovics, Stephano: "La basilica di S. Quirino nell'antica Savaria." *Corvina,* 1938. The excavations have been continued in the past years by Tihamér Szentléleky.

17. Gerő, László: "Az Óbuda–Király-hegyen feltárt római katonai amfiteátrum helyreállítása" [The Restoration of the Roman Military Amphitheatre Excavated in Óbuda–Királyhegy]. *Technika* 1941. No. 8; with abstract in German and Italian.

18. Héjj, Miklós: *The Royal Palace of Visegrád.* Budapest, 1969. Published also in German and French.

19. The first excavation and conservation were carried out by Kálmán Lux; further excavations were performed by István Méri; the restoration is the work of Ferenc Erdei. The iconography of the frescoes was established by Marianne H. Sallay.

20. Dercsényi, Dezső: "Tutela dei monumenti in Ungheria dopo la liberazione". *Accta Historiae Artium* II (1954), pp. 99–134. Dercsényi, Dezső: *Tíz év magyar műemlékvédelem* [Ten Years of the Preservation of Historical Monuments in Hungary]. *Magyar Műemlékvédelem 1949–1959.* Budapest, 1960. pp. 9–38; with full German translation. Dercsényi, Dezső: "Ungarische Denkmalpflege nach dem zweiten Weltkriege." *Österreichische Zeitschrift für Kunst und Denkmalpflege* XV (1961), pp. 125–156. Entz, Géza: "La tutale dei monumenti negli ultimi tre anni." *Acta Historiae Artium* V (1957), pp. 255–282. Dercsényi, Dezső: "La tutela dei monumenti in Ungheria negli ultimi otto anni." *Acta Historiae Artium* XIV (1966), pp. 1–39. Also in *Information Hungary* Budapest and London: The Pergamon Press, 1968, pp. 160–167.

21. As an initial step, we should mention the elaboration of the National Building Regulations (1960); Volume I on urban development and the preservation of historical monuments also contains detailed operative measures. The next step was the forming of the Building Act (Act 1964. IV.) which, completing Law 13/1949, determined the categories of preservation and organically incorporated all activities in this field within the scope of building affairs. On the basis of this Act and Decision 30/1964 of the Council of Ministers, the Ministry of Works issued Decree No. 1 of 1967, which may be considered as the detailed code of preservation of historical monuments in Hungary. Beyond questions of legislation, the close connection developed between construction affairs and the preservation of historical monuments has brought significant changes in the whole organization of the Works portfolio. The biggest designing offices have set up special sections for the preservation of historical monuments whose work was not confined to actual restorations: the respective section of Budapest Town Planning Office, for instance, also took part, under the direction of Frigyes Pogány, in the solution of theoretical problems and the elaboration of methods of classification. The most important planning section concerned with historical monuments is operating even today within the framework of the Scientific and Planning Institute for Town Development.

22. In spite of the difficulties encountered in this field, the listing of

buildings of architectural or historical interest and their declaration as historical monuments was started at an early date. Péter Gerecze published his work entitled "A műemlékek helyrajzi jegyzéke és irodalma" [Topographical List and Literature of Historical Monuments] as Volume II of the series *Magyar Műemlékek* [Historical Monuments of Hungary] edited by Gyula Forster as early as 1906. Although the book describes our historical monuments only up to 1711 (the date of the peace treaty concluding Rákóczi's War of Independence) the literary references contained in it make it a useful manual even today. The continuation of this work, coinciding with similar activities initiated in other European countries, followed only half a century later. Genthon, István: *Magyarország műemlékei* [Historical Monuments of Hungary]. Budapest, 1951. Second edition, enlarged with illustrations and bibliography: *Magyarország Művészeti Emlékei* [Monuments of Art in Hungary]. Vol. I–III. Budapest, 1959–1961.

23. The methods of surveying townscape and historical monuments have been elaborated by Imre Papp, László Gerő and István Kisléghi Nagy. The surveying of about 70 settlements were completed.

24. From the series entitled *Magyarország műemléki topográfiája* [Topographical List of Hungarian Historical Monuments] the following have appeared so far:
Vol. I. *Esztergom* Part I., Museums, Treasury, Library. Budapest, 1948.
Vol. II. *Sopron és környéke műemlékei* [The Historical Monuments of Sopron and its Environment]. Budapest, 1953. 2nd enlarged edition: Budapest, 1956.
Vol. III. *Nógrád megye műemlékei* [The Historical Monuments of the County of Nógrád]. Budapest, 1954. Vol. IV. *Budapest műemlékei*. I. [The Historical Monuments of Budapest]. Part I. Budapest, 1955. Vol. V. *Pest megye műemlékei* I–II [The Historical Monuments of the County of Pest. Parts I–II. Budapest, 1958. Vol. VI. *Budapest műemlékei* II. [The Historical Monuments of Budapest]. Part II. Budapest, 1962. *Heves megye műemlékei* I. [Historical Monuments of Heves County]. Budapest, 1969. Cf. Entz, Géza: "10 Jahre Kunsttopografie." *Acta Historiae Artium* IX (1963), pp. 393–396.

25. Two series have been started. In the first edited by the author of this book, the description of the historical monuments follows the art historical development of the town; the second, edited by Imre Papp, also includes a detailed townscape analysis.

26. Four editions of this yearbook of the National Inspectorate have appeared so far. The first: *Magyar Műemlékvédelem 1949–1959* [Preservation of Historical Monuments in Hungary in 1949–1959]. Budapest, 1960, summarized the works carried out in the first ten years. The following two contained the material of two years each (*Magyar Műemlékvédelem 1959–1960*. Budapest, 1964, and *Magyar Műemlékvédelem 1961–1962*. Budapest, 1967. The latest volume: *Magyar Műemlékvédelem 1963–1967*. Budapest, 1968, also reviews several years' work. The studies are published with abstracts and lists of the illustrations in German.

27. Horler, Miklós: "A műemlékvédelem elméleti kérdéseiről" [On the Theoretical Problems of the Preservation of Historical Monuments]. *Építés- és Közlekedéstudományi Közlemények* VIII (1964), pp. 265–293; with German abstract. Gerő, László: "A magyar műemlékvédelem problematikája" [The Problems of Monument Preservation in Hungary]. *Építés- és Közlekedéstudományi Közlemények* II (1958), pp. 425–444. Horler, Miklós: "A műemlékek

helyreállítási irányelvei" [The Principles of the Restoration of Historical Monuments]. *Építés- és Közlekedéstudományi Közlemények XI* (1968), pp. 447–460.

28. The protection of historic towns and town centres has been discussed at several conferences of the Academies of Sciences of socialist countries (Erfurt, 1956; Dobris, 1957; Warsaw, 1959). Cf. Gerő, László: "A városépítéstörténet és építés történeti városokban c. akadémiai munkaközösség első, második és harmadik nemzetközi konferenciája" [The First, Second and Third International Conferences of the Academic Team on "The History of Town Building and Building in Historic Towns"]. *Építés- és Közlekedéstudományi Közlemények* (1961), pp. 243–278. The fourth conference was held in Budapest in 1962. Its material, with a lengthy German abstract, has been published in the *Építés- és Közlekedéstudományi Közlemények* VIII (1964), pp. 5–399. Cf. Gerő, László: "Műemléki jelentőségű területek rendezésének metodikai kérdései" [Methodical Questions in the Development of Areas of Historical or Architectural Interest]. *Építés- és Közlekedéstudományi Közlemények*, VII (1963) pp. 3–20. A study with abstract in German and with plans of all the protected towns in Hungary. Granasztói, Pál: "Történeti városközpontjaink reorganizációjának jellegzetes kérdése." [Specific Problems in the Reorganization of Our Historic Town Centres]. *Építés- és Közlekedéstudományi Közlemények* (1964), pp. 37–84. Also in German.

29. "A velencei carta és a magyar műemlékvédelem" [The Venice Carta and the Preservation of Historical Monuments in Hungary]. A publication of the Hungarian Section of the ICOMOS. Vol. I. Budapest, 1967, with abstract in French.

30. Gerő, László: "A Balaton régió műemléki helyreállítása" [Restoration of the Historical Monuments in the Region of Lake Balaton]. *Építés- és Közlekedéstudományi Közlemények* VIII (1964), pp. 45–46, with abstract in German.

31. UNESCO Executive Board, Seventy-Second Session: "The Preservation of Monuments and Other Cultural Property in Association with the Development of Tourism." Report by the Director-General.

32. Architect: Egon Pfannl; archaeologist: Klára Póczy.

33. Architects: László Hegyi and Egon Pfannl; archaeologist: István Wellner.

34. Hajnóczy, Gyula–H. Vladár, Ágnes: "Aquincum polgárváros műemléki helyreállításának távlati terve" [Long-range Plan for the Restoration of the Civic Town of Aquincum]. *Műemlékvédelem* 1962, pp. 206–211; with abstract in French.

35. Architect: Egon Pfannl; archaeologists: Lajos Nagy and Melinda Kaba. Cf. Antal Czétényi: "A Raktár utcai *cella trichora* helyreállítása" [The Restoration of the Raktár Street *cella trichora*]. *Műemlékvédelem* 1962, pp. 212–214; with abstract in French. Kaba, Melinda: "Az aquincumi *cella trichora* újabb helyreállítása" [The Further Restoration of the *cella trichora* in Aquincum]. *Budapest Régiségei* XXI (1964), pp. 337–343; with abstract in German.

36. Hajnóczy, Gyula—Szentléleky, Tihamér: *Római kori homlokzathelyreállítás Szombathelyen* [The Restoration of a Roman Façade in Szombathely]. *Magyar Műemlékvédelem* 1959–1960. Budapest, 1964, pp. 129–326; with abstract in German. The two authors were also respectively the designer and archaeologist of the restoration.

37. Radnóti, Aladár: "Une église du haut moyen âge" and Dercsényi, Dezső: "L'église de Privina à Zalavár" *Études slaves et romaines* 1948, pp. 21–30, 75–100, respectively, Cs. Sós, Ágnes: "Über die Fragen des frühmittelalterlichen Kirchenbaues in Mosapurc-Zalavár." *Acta Congr. Historiae Slavicae Salisburgensis in memoriam Cirilli et Methodii*. Wiesbaden, 1966, pp. 69–86.

38. Architect: Tibor Koppány; archaeologist: Ilona Valter.

39. Éri, István—Gerő Kramer, Márta—Szentléleky, Tihamér: "A dörgicsei középkori templomromok" [The Medieval Church Ruins in Dörgicse]. *Magyar Műemlékvédelem* 1959–1960. Budapest, 1964, pp. 95–116; with abstract in German. The restoration was designed by Tibor Koppány; archaeologist: István Éri; art historian: Márta Gerő Krámer.

40. Architect: Tibor Koppány; archaeologist: Ilona Sz. Czeglédy.

41. Architect: Tibor Koppány; archaeologist: István Éri. Cf. Koppány, Tibor: *A nagyvázsonyi pálos kolostor romjainak konzerválása* [Conservation of the Ruins of the Paulite Monastery in Nagyvázsony]. *Magyar Műemlékvédelem* 1961–1962. Budapest, 1966, pp. 103–110; with abstract in German.

42. Architects: Ferenc Erdei and Tibor Koppány; archeaologist: Katalin H. Gyürky. Cf. "A veszprémi Szt. György kápolna romjainak állagvédelme" [The Conservation of the Ruins of St. George's Chapel in Veszprém]. *Műemlékvédelem* 1961, pp. 89–92; with abstract in German. H. Gyürky, Katalin: "Die St. Georg–Kapelle in der Burg von Veszprém." *Acta Archaeologica* 15 (1963), pp. 344–408.

43. Entz, Géza: "A tudományos kutatás szerepe a romok műemléki védelmében" [The Role of Research Work in the Preservation of Ruins]. *Építés- és Közlekedéstudományi Közlemények* X (1964), pp. 7–13; with abstract in German. Entz, Géza: *A korszerű régészeti kutatások szerepe a műemlékvédelemben*. [The Role of Modern Archaeological Explorations in the Preservation of Historical Monuments]. *Magyar Műemlékvédelem* 1961–1962. Budapest, 1964, pp. 7–22; with abstract in German. In 1964 the Hungarian Academy of Sciences organized an international conference on the preservation of historical monuments. The key question discussed was the preservation of ruins. The material of the conference appeared in *Építés- és Közlekedéstudományi Közlemények* X (1966), pp. 3–177.

44. Gerő, László: *Váraink védelme* [The Protection of Our Castles]. *Magyar Műemlékvédelem* 1949–1959. Budapest, pp. 77–96; with abstract in German. Horler, Miklós "Várromok restaurálásának módszertani kérdései" [Technical Questions Associated with the Restoration of the Ruins of Castles]. *Építés- és Közlekedéstudományi Közlemények* X (1966), pp. 13–20; with abstract in German. Sedlmayr, János: "Középkori várak helyreállítása Magyarországon" [The Restoration of Medieval Castles in Hungary]. *Építés- és Közlekedéstudományi Közlemények* X. (1966), pp. 21–38; with abstract in German. Gerő, László: *Castles in Hungary*. Budapest, 1969.

45. Architects: László Gerő, Károly Ferenczy; archaeologists: József Komáromy, Erzsébet Lócsy, Ilona Sz. Czeglédy, Miklós Héjj; sculptor-restorer: Ernő Szakál.

46. Architect: Tibor Koppány; archaeologist: Károly Kozák.

47. Architect: János Sedlmayr; archaeologist: István Éri. Éri, István: "Beszámoló a nagyvázsonyi Kinizsi vár helyreállításáról" [A Report on the Restoration of the Castle of Kinizsi at Nagyvázsony]. *Műemlékvédelem* 1958, pp. 2–22; with abstract in French.

48. Architect: Ferenc Erdei; archaeologist: Mária G. Sándor. Cf. Erdei, Ferenc: "A vártgesztesi vár helyreállítása" [The Restoration of the Castle of Vártgesztes]. *Műemlékvédelem* 1965, pp. 204–211; with abstract in French.

49. Architects: Középülettervező Vállalat [Enterprise for the Planning of Public Buildings] (István Janáki, Lajos Hidasi, László Gerő); archaeologist: Budapesti Történeti Múzeum [Budapest Historical Museum] (László Gerevich). Gerő, László: *A budai vár helyreállítása* [The Restoration of the Castle of Buda]. Budapest, 1951. Gerevich, László: *A budai vár feltárása* [The Excavation of the Castle of Buda]. Budapest, 1966, with abstract in German. Czagány, István: *A Budavári Palota és a Szent György téri épületek* [The Royal Palace of Buda and the Buildings of St. George's Place]. Budapest, 1966.

50. Architect: Ferenc Erdei; archaeologist: Nándor Parádi. Cf. Parádi, Nándor: *A gyulai vár ásatásának építéstörténeti eredményei* [The Results of the Excavation of the Castle of Gyula]. *Magyar Műemlékvédelem*. 1961–1962. Budapest, 1966, pp.135–166; with abstract in German.

51. Architects: László Gerő (chapel), Károly Ferenczy, Tamás Dragonits; archaeologists: László Papp, Valéria Kovács, Ilona Sz. Czeglédy; art historian: András Gergelyffy. The restoration of the bay-window was designed by Ernő Szakál. Cf. Ferenczy, Károly—Sz. Czeglédy, Ilona: "A siklósi vár" [The Castle of Siklós]. *Műemlékvédelem* 1966, pp. 76–84; with abstract in French. Gerő, László: "A siklósi vár helyreállítása" [The Restoration of the Castle of Siklós]. *Építés- és Közlekedéstudományi Közlemények* II, (1957), pp. 385–416; with abstract in German.

52. Architect: Mihály Détshy; archaeologist: Károly Kozák. Cf. Détshy, M., Kozák, K.: *Az egri várban álló gótikus palota helyreállítása* [The Restoration of the Gothic Palace in the Castle of Eger]. *Magyar Műemlékvédelem* 1959–1960. Budapest, 1964, pp. 31–72; with abstract in German.

53. Architect: János Sedlmayr; archaeologist: Imre Holl; art historian: András Gergelyffi. Cf. Sedlmayer, János: "A kőszegi Jurisich vár helyreállítása" [The Restoration of the Jurisich Castle of Kőszeg]. *Műemlékvédelem* 1958, pp. 143–148, 1965, pp. 65–77: with abstract in French.

54. Architects: László Gerő, László Borsos, Mihály Détshy, Tibor Koppány; archaeologists: Julia Kovalovszky, Vera Molnár. Cf. Détshy, Mihály: *A sárospataki vár helyreállítási munkái 1955–1962-ben* [The Restoration of the Castle of Sárospatak in 1955–1962]. *Magyar Műemlékvédelem* 1961–1962. Budapest, 1966, pp. 67–88; with abstract in German.

55. Architect: Tamás Dragonits; archaeologist: Emese S. Nagy; art historian: András Gergelyffy. Cf. Dragonits, Tamás: "Az egervári kastély" [The Castle of Egervár]. *Műemlékvédelem* 1966, pp. 218–225; with abstract in French.

56. Ferenczy, Károly: *Kastélyok felhasználása és helyreállítása* [The Restoration and Utilization of Country Palaces and Manor Houses]. *Magyar Műemlékvédelem* 1949–1959. Budapest, 1960, pp. 55–64; with abstract in German.

57. Architect: Jenő Rados.

58. Architect: Judit Nagypál; art historian: Marianna Sallay. Restoration of the *sgraffiti:* János Illés and Róza Szentesi. Cf. Nagypál, Judit: "A pácini reneszánsz kastély helyreállítása" [The Restoration of the Renaissance Manor House of Pácin]. *Műemlékvédelem* 1964, pp. 233–241; with abstract in French.

59. Architect: Antal Thomas.

60. Architect: Sándor Hevesi. Restoration of the mural paintings: Endre Fenyő.

61. Architect: István Péteri.

62. Architect: Jenő Rados.

63. Architect: László Ágostházi; restoration of mural paintings: István Lente and colleagues.

64. Architect: László Borsos. The mural paintings have been uncovered and restored by Loránd Sárdy.

65. Architects: Jenő Rados, István Vargha. The *chinoiserie* mural paintings were restored by Loránd Sárdy and colleagues, the frescoes of the state room by Antal Borsa. Cf. Cs. Katona, Imre: "A fertődi (Esterházy) kastély kialakulása" [The Development of the Fertőd (Esterházy) Castle]. *Építés- és Közlekedéstudományi Közlemények* III (1959), pp. 77–130; with abstract in German.

66. Péczely, Béla: *Középületek helyreállítása* [The Restoration of Public Buildings]. *Magyar Műemlékvédelem* 1949–1959. Budapest, 1960, pp. 43–54; with abstract in German.

67. Architects: Béla Országh, László Ágostházi.

68. Architect: László Borsos.

69. Architect: Károly Ferenczy; art historians: József Csemegi, Éva Hárs. Entz, Géza: "A Káptalan utca 2. középkori ház Pécsett" [The Medieval House at No. 2, Káptalan Street in Pécs]. *Műemlékvédelem* 1958, pp. 72–78; with abstract in French.

70. Architect: Jenő Kismarty Lechner.

71. The restoration of the Martinelli Square business house was designed by Zoltán Vass.

72. Dümmerling, Ödön—Détshy, Mihály—Császár, László—Kuthy, Sándor: *Egyházi műemlékeink helyreállítása* [The Restoration of Our Ecclesiastical Monuments]. *Magyar Műemlékvédelem* 1949–1959. Budapest, 1960, pp. 97–120; with abstract in German.

73. Architect: Ferenc Mendele; archaeologist: Ilona Sz. Czeglédy; art historian: Géza Entz.

74. Architect: Ferenc Erdei; art historian: Ida Ratkai.

75. Arhitect: Ferenc Erdei; archaeologist: Béla Kovács. Cf. Erdei, Ferenc—Kovács, Béla: "A váraszói románkori templom feltárása és helyreállítása" [The Excavation and Restoration of the Roman Church at Váraszó] *Az Egri Múzeum Évkönyve* II (1964), pp. 181–220; with abstract in German.

76. Architect: László Gerő; archaeologist: Miklós Héjj.

77. Architect: Tibor Koppány; art historian: Marianna Sallay.

78. Architect: Jenő Rados; archaeologist: Ilona Valter; art historian:

András Gergelyffy; sculptural restoration Ernő Szakál. Cf. András Gergelyffy: "L'Église abbatiale de Bélapátfalva." *Acta Historiae Artium* VI (1959), pp. 245–276.

79. Architect: Ödön Dümmerling. Cf. Dümmerling, Ödön: "La Restauration de l'église Saint-Pierre et Saint-Paul à Sopronhorpács." *Cahiers de Civilisation Médiévale* (1962), pp. 193–194.

80. Architect: Judit Nagypál; archaeologist: Vera Molnár; art historian: Marianna Sallay. Cf. Gervers Veronika: "The Romaresque Church of Karcsa." *Gesta VII* (1968). pp. 36–47.

81. Architect: Ferenc Erdei; archaeologist: István Éri; art historian: Sándor Tóth. Cf. Pevsner, Nikolaus: "Impression of Hungarian Building." *The New Hungarian Quarterly* VII (1966), No. 21., p. 47.

82. Architect: Tibor Koppány; archaeologist: Ilona Sz. Czeglédy; art historian: Anna Jakubik. Cf. Koppány, Tibor—Sz. Czeglédy, Ilona: "Beszámoló a mátraverebélyi rk. templom helyreállításáról" [Report on the Restoration of the Roman Catholic Church at Mátraverebély]. *Műemlékvédelem* 1963, pp. 65–72; with abstract in French.

83. Architect: Károly Ferenczy; archaeologist: Vera Molnár. Cf. Molnár, Vera.: "Beszámoló a sárospataki rk. templom 1964–1965 évi ásatásáról." [Report on the 1964–1965 Excavation of the Roman Catholic Church of Sárospatak]. *Műemlékvédelem* 1966, pp. 226–233; with abstract in French. Molnár, Vera: "A sárospataki *rotundáról*" [The Sárospatak Rotunda]. *A Móra Ferenc Múzeum Évkönyve* II (1966–1967), Szeged, 1968, pp. 153–158; with abstract in French.

84. Architect: Zsuzsa Sedlmayr Beck; art historian: Géza Entz.

85. Architect: János Sedlmayr; archaeologist: István Éri. Cf. Sedlmayr, János: "A nagyvázsonyi Szent István templom helyreállítása" [The Restoration of St. Stephen's Church at Nagyvázsony]. *Műemlékvédelem* 1962, pp. 1–7; with abstract in French.

86. The work had been carried out under the direction of the sculptor–restorer, Ernő Szakál. Cf. Szakál, Ernő: "A sopronbánfalvi gótikus templom helyreállításáról" [The Restoration of the Gothic Church of Sopronbánfalva. *Műemlékvédelem* 1959, pp. 75–82; with abstract in French.

87. Architect: János Sedlmayr; archaeologist: Ilona Sz. Czeglédy. Concerning the painted wooden ceiling, cf. R. Tombor, Ilona: Old Hungarian Painted Woodwork. Budapest, 1967. Published also in German and French.

88. Architect: Ilona Sch. Pusztai; archaeologist: Éva Kozák. Restoration of the mural paintings by Ferenc Rádi.

89. Architects: László Gerő and Kálmán Lux; sculptor–restorer: Ernő Szakál; painter–restorer: László Bartha.

90. Architect: János Sedlmayr; art historian: Marianna H. Sallay. Cf. H. Sallay, Marianna—Sedlmayr, János: *A soproni középkori zsinagóga* [The Medieval Synagogue in Sopron]. *Magyar Műemlékvédelem* 1959–1960, pp. 191–206; with abstract in German. Scheiber, Alexandre: "La Découverte d'une synagogue médiévale à Sopron." *Revue des Études Juives* XIII (1959–1960). I., pp. 81–87.

91. Architect: Andor Nendvich.

92. Architect: Károly Ferenczy; archaeologist Győző Gerő.

93. Architect: Károly Ferenczy; archaeologist: Győző Gerő.

94. Architect: Egon Pfannl; archaeologist: Győző Gerő.

95. Architect of the restoration of Rudas Bath: György Tőkés; archaeologist: Győző Gerő. Architect of the restoration of Király Bath: Egon Pfannl; archaeologist: Győző Gerő. Borsos, Béla: "Királyfürdő" [The Király Bath). *Építés- és Közlekedéstudományi Közlemények* I (1967), pp. 69–112; with abstract in German.

96. Architects: Kálmán Lux, László Gerő, László Borsos.

97. Architect: Géza Hell.

98. Architect: Mihály Détshy.

99. Voit, Pál: *Szentendre*. 1968. Published in German, English and French.

100. Sedlmayr, János: *Műemléki lakóházak helyreállítása* The Restoration of Listed Dwelling Houses]. *Magyar Műemlékvédelem* 1949–1959. Budapest, 1960; with abstract in German.

101. Regarding the restoration of dwelling houses in Buda, see Horler, N.: "La Reconstruction du centre historique de Buda." *Monumentum* 1967. pp. 25–51; with abstract in English. Gerő, L.: *Gothic Houses in Buda*. 1966. Published also in French and German.

102. Architect: Zsuzsa Sedlmayr Beck.

103. Architect: Ferenc Mendele.

104. Architect: Ferenc Mendele. Cf. Tóth, János: "Az utolsó magyarországi hajómalom" [The Last of the Ship-mills of Hungary]. *Műemlékvédelem* 1965, pp. 212–216; with abstract in French.

105. Architect: Ferenc Mendele. Cf. Mendele, Ferenc: "A kiskunhalasi műemléki szélmalom helyreállítása" [The Restoration of the Wind-mill at Kiskunhalas]. *Technikatörténeti Szemle* IV (1967), pp. 209–230; with abstract in German and English.

106. Tóth, János : *Népi építészetünk hagyományai* [The Traditions of Hungarian Rural Architecture]. Budapest, 1961, with abstract in French. Vargha, László: "A népi építészet – a néprajzi jellegű műemlékek—regionális kérdései " [Regional Problems of Rural Architecture and the Preservation of Buildings of Ethnographic Interest]. *Építés- és Közlekedéstudományi Közlemények* X (1964), pp. 155–167, with abstract in German. Vargha, L. – Cseh, I. – Tóth, J.: "Népi és ipari emlékek védelme" [The Protection of Rural and Industrial Relics]. *Műemlékvédelem* 1949, pp.121–144, with abstract in German.

107. Architects: István Cseh, Ferenc Mendele, Kálmán Tóth.

108. Tóth, János: *Göcsej népi építészete* [Rural Architecture in Göcsej] Budapest, 1965, with abstract in French. Outhouses designed by Mária Waigand; enclosed houses by Erzsébet C. Harrach.

109. Architects: András Román, Ferenc Mendele. Cf. by same architects: "Egy népi műemlék helyreállítása" [The Restoration of a Rural Relic]. *Műemlékvédelem* 1965, pp. 107–110, with abstract in French.

110. Architect: Ferenc Mendele.

111. Architect: László Gerő.

112. Architect: István Cseh. Cf. "A nemesvámosi csárda helyreállítása" [The Restoration of the Village Inn at Nemesvámos]. *Műemlékvédelem* 1967, p. 37.

113. Architect: István Cseh.

114. Architect: Ferenc Mendele.
Cf. Mendele, Ferenc "A pankaszi harangláb műemléki helyreállítása" [The Restoration of the Belfry at Pankasz]. *Savaria. A Vas megyei múzeumok értesítője*, 3 (1965); Szombathely (1966), pp. 229–236, with abstract in German.

115. Szakál, Ernő: *Kő- és faszobrászati helyreálllítások* [The Restoration of Stone and Wood Sculpture]. *Magyar Műemlékvédelem* 1949–1959. Budapest, 1960, pp. 145–154; with abstract in German.

116. Szakál, Ernő: "Díszkutak a visegrádi királyi palotában" [Fountains in the Royal Palace of Visegrád]. *Műemlékvédelem* 1966, pp. 28–36, with abstract in French. Szakál, Ernő: "Gótikus erkély a siklósi várban" [Gothic Bay-window of the Castle of Siklós]. *Műemlékvédelem* 1966, pp. 84–86, with abstract in French.

117. Cf. Dercsényi, Dezső: "Hozzászólás Gerő László: 'A magyar műemlékvédelem problematikája' c. előadásához" [Contribution to L. Gerő's Lecture on 'The Problems of the Protection of Historical Monuments in Hungary']. *Építés- és Közlekedéstudományi Közlemények* II. évf., pp. 425–476, with abstract in German.

118. Entz, G.–Szakál, E.: "La Reconstitution du sarcophage du roi Étienne." *Acta Historiae Artium* X (1964), pp. 215–228.

119. Dercsényi, Dezső: *A pécsi kőtár* [The Pécs Lapidary Museum]. Pécs, 1962, with abstract in French.

120. Restored by Kálmán Németh.
Cf. Baranyai, H.: "Der Krucsay-Altar in Nyírbátor." *Acta Historiae Artium* VI (1959), pp. 355–372.

121. With the exception of the Sárospatak altars, which had been restored in the workshop of the Arts Fund, the restoration of the altars was performed in the workshop of the National Inspectorate of Historical Monuments under the direction of Endre Ujlaky.

122. An excellent work of János Illés and his colleagues.

123. The work at Székesfehérvár was done by Endre Fenyő, that at Sümeg by István Przudzik.

1. ZSÁMBÉK
2. VESZPRÉM
3. BÉLAPÁTFALVA
4. FERTŐD
5. BALÁCAPUSZTA
6. ZALAVÁR
7. TÁKOS
8. TÚRISTVÁNDI
9. TISZACSÉCSE
10. MÁNDOK
11. SZAMOSTATÁRFALVA
12. CSENGER
13. SOPRONBÁNFALVA
14. SZOMBATHELY
15. JÁK
16. SZALAFŐ
17. VELEMÉR
18. VITKA
19. KŐSZEG
20. SOPRON
21. TIHANY
22. HEGYMAGAS
23. GYŐR
24. NAGYVÁZSONY
25. SIKLÓS
26. PÉCS
27. KESZTHELY
28. SZENTENDRE
29. EGER
30. FELDEBRŐ
31. RÁCKEVE
32. SÁROSPATAK
33. DIÓSGYŐR
34. PÁCIN
35. SZÉKESFEHÉRVÁR
36. FELSŐÖRS
37. VÁC
38. VISEGRÁD
39. DÖRGICSE
40. BADACSONY
41. ESZTERGOM
42. SÜMEG
43. NAGYBÖRZSÖNY
44. NÓGRÁDSÁP
45. GYULA
46. NYÍRBÁTOR
47. PANNONHALMA
48. FERTŐRÁKOS
49. VÁRASZÓ
50. VERPELÉT
51. VÁRGESZTES
52. ECSER
53. NEMESVÁMOS
54. MÁTRAVEREBÉLY
55. ALSÓÖRS
56. EGREGY
57. EGERVÁR
58. FENÉKPUSZTA

Plates

1. Budapest, III (Óbuda):
Military Amphitheatre in Nagyszombat Street. Middle of 2nd century

2. Budapest, III (Óbuda):
Ruins of the civilian town of Aquincum. 2nd to 4th century

3. Szombathely: Mosaics in the imperial palace (?). Early 4th century

4. Szombathely: The imperial palace (?). Early 4th century
5. Szombathely: Mosaics in the imperial palace (?). Early 4th century

6. Szombathely: The Isis Shrine. Late 2nd century
7. Szombathely: Roman road

8. Szombathely: Relief from the Isis Shrine. Late 2nd century

9. Szombathely: Relief from the Isis Shrine. Late 2nd century

10. Székesfehérvár: Foundation walls of the royal Basilica. 11th century

11. Felsődörgicse: Ruins of the Roman Catholic Church. 13th century
12. Feldebrő: Roman Catholic Church. The crypt. 11th century

13. Ecsér: Ruins of the Roman Catholic Church. 13th century

15. Zsámbék: Aisle of the Premonstratensian Church. 13th century

14. Zsámbék: Ruins of the Premonstratensian Church. 13th century

16. Nagyvázsony: Ruins of the Paulite Monastery. 15th century

17. Esztergom: The Royal Palace. 12th to 13th century

18. Esztergom: The Chapel
and the door to the Royal Palace.
About 1200

19. Esztergom: Interior view of the Chapel. About 1200

20. Visegrád: The keep, called Solomon's Tower, in 1865. Mid-13th century

21. Visegrád: Solomon's Tower in 1922. Mid-13th century

22. Visegrád: The restored upper hall in Solomon's Tower
23. Visegrád: Solomon's Tower after restoration

24. Visegrád: The Gothic cloisters surrounding the court of honour of the Royal Palace. 15th century

25. Visegrád: The court of honour of the Royal Palace. 14th to 15th century

26. Castle of Sümeg. 14th to 17th century
27. Nagyvázsony:
The Kinizsi Castle. 15th century

28. Castle of Diósgyőr. 14th
to 17th century

29. Castle of Gyula. 14th to 15th century

30. Castle of Várgesztes. 14th to 15th century
31. Castle of Siklós. 14th to 18th century
32. Siklós: The Chapel of the Castle. 15th century

33. Budapest: The former Royal Palace. 15th to 19th century

34. Budapest: The Castle Chapel. 15th century

35. Budapest: Hall of the Castle. 15th century

36. Eger: The former episcopal residence in the Castle. 15th century

37. Castle of Kőszeg. 15th century

38. Kőszeg: Staircase in the Castle
39. Kőszeg: Tavern in the Zwinger

40. Kőszeg: The bail of the Castle

41. Kőszeg: Passage in the Castle

42. Sárospatak: View of the Rákóczi Castle from the bank of the river Bodrog. 13th to 16th century

43. Sárospatak:
The bail of the Rákóczi Castle

44–45. Pácin: *Sgraffito* from the façade of the manor house. 16th century
46. The Pácin Manor House. 16th century

47. Budapest, XXII (Nagytétény): Manor House. 18th century
48. Sümeg: The Episcopal Palace. 18th century
49. The Palace of Eugène of Savoy at Ráckeve. 1702

50. Manor House at Fertőrákos. 18th century

51. Castle at Egervár. 16th century

52. Fertőd: The Esterházy Palace. Second half of 18th century

53. Fertőd: Garden wing of the Esterházy Palace. Second half of 18th century
54. Fertőd· "Sala terrena" in the Esterházy Palace. Second half of 18th century

55. Fertőd: Main front of the Esterházy Palace. Second half of 18th century

56. Eger: Lyceum
Second half of 18th century
57. Veszprém: The Episcopal Palace.
Second half of 18th century

58. Szombathely: The Episcopal Palace. Second half of 18th century

59. Budapest: The County Hall. Early 19th century

60. Budapest: The Vigadó (Municipal Music Hall). Middle of 19th century

61. Budapest: The National Museum. First half of 19th century

62. Pécs: No. 2. Káptalan Street. Gothic window

63. Pécs: No. 2. Káptalan Street. Front view. 15th to 18th century

64. Pécs: The Cathedral at the end of the 18th century. Engraving by Koller.

65. Pécs: The Cathedral after reconstruction by Mihály Pollack. First half of the 19th century

66. Pécs: The Cathedral in the townscape
67. Pécs: Front view of the Cathedral after reconstruction at the end of the 19th century

68. Pannonhalma: The *Porta Speciosa* of the Benedictine Abbey
after restoration. 13th century

69. Door to the calefactory
of the Benedictine Abbey Church at
Pannonhalma. 13th to 15th century
70. The Cloisters of the Benedictine Abbey
at Pannonhalma. 15th century

71. Bélapátfalva: Cistercian Abbey Church. Mid-13th century

72. Bélapátfalva: Interior view of the Cistercian Abbey Church

73. Felsőörs: Interior of the Provostal Church. 13th century

74. Felsőörs: Provostal Church. Front view. 13th century

77. The Benedictine Abbey Church after restoration

75. Ják: Benedictine Abbey Church. The nave. Built prior to 1256

76. The Benedictine Abbey Church before restoration. Built prior to 1256

78. Egregy: Roman Catholic Church. 13th century
79. Velemér: Roman Catholic Church. 13th century
80. Váraszó: Roman Catholic Church. 13th century

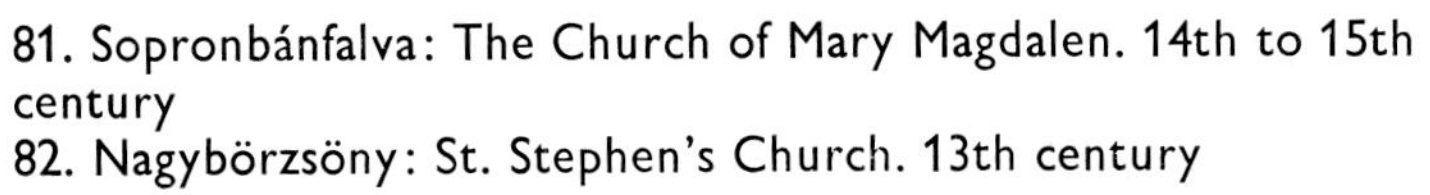

81. Sopronbánfalva: The Church of Mary Magdalen. 14th to 15th century
82. Nagybörzsöny: St. Stephen's Church. 13th century

83. Nógrádsáp: Roman Catholic Church. 14th to 15th century

84. Nógrádsáp: Roman Catholic Church. Interior. 15th century

85. **Budapest**: The Matthias Church before restoration

86. Budapest: The Matthias Church today
87. Budapest: Matthias Church with Szentháromság Square

88. Mátraverebély: Roman Catholic Church. Interior. 14th to 15th century
89. Mátraverebély: Roman Catholic Church. 14th to 15th century

90. Nagybörzsöny: The Miners' Church. 15th century

93. Nyírbátor: Calvinist Church. Interior. 15th century

91. Nagyvázsony: St. Stephen's Church. 15th century

92. Nyírbátor: Calvinist Church. 15th century

94. Sopronbánfalva: The sanctuary of the former Paulite Church. 16th century
95. Interior of the Calvinist Church at Tákos. 18th century

97. Mándok: Calvinist Church. 18th century

96. Csenger: Calvinist Church. 15th century

98. Sopron: The former Chapter Hall of the Franciscan Monastery.
14th century

99. Sopron: Medieval Synagogue.
14th century

100. Pécs: *Turbé* of Idris Baba. 16th century

101. Pécs: Belvárosi (Downtown) Roman Catholic Church. Former *djami* of Ghazi Kasim pasha. 16th century

102. Pécs: *Djami* of Yakovali Hassan. 16th century

103. Budapest:
Király Bath. 16th to 19th century

104. Szigetvár:
Interior of the Suleiman *djami*.
1566.

105. Budapest:
University Church. 18th century

106. Budapest: St. Anna's Church. 18th century
107. Budapest: Belvárosi (Pest City) Parish Church. 15th to 18th century

108. Eger: Former Church of the Minorites. 18th century

109. Szombathely: Cathedral. Late 18th century

110. Ráckeve:
Greek Catholic Church. 15th century

111. Szentendre: The Belgrade Cathedral.
Middle of 18th century

112. Szentendre: The Blagoveštenska
or Greek Church.
Middle of 18th century

113. Budapest: Buda townscape

114. Budapest, I: No. 31 Úri Street. 15th century
115. Budapest, I: No. 2 Országház Street. 15th century
116. Budapest, I: Courtyard of No. 18–20 Országház Street

117. Sopron: View of the town

118. Sopron: No. 5 Kolostor Street. 15th to 18th century

119. Sopron: View of the town

120. Túristvándi: Water-mill. 19th century

121. Újmassa: Foundry. About 1820

122. Verpelét: Smithery. 18th century

123. Tihany: Peasant house. 19th century

124. Tiszacsécse: Peasant house. 19th century

125. Hegymagas: The Tarányi press-house. 18th century

126. Szamostatárfalva:
The wooden belfry of the Calvinist Church. 18th century
127. Szalafő: Outhouse. 19th century

128. Badacsony: Róza Szegedy house. 18th century

129. Visegrád: Royal Palace.
Lions' Fountain. 15th century

130. Visegrád:
The wall-fountain of Louis I. 14th century.
Budapest. National Museum
131. Visegrád: The Angevin well-house.
Late 14th century

132. Tihany: Former Benedictine Monastery. Lapidary Museum

133. Pécs: The *Lapidarium*

134. Pécs: *Lapidarium*. The Altar of the Holy Cross. 12th century

135. Győr: The Ark of the Covenant. 18th century

136. Nyírbátor: The Krucsay Altar of the former Church of the Minorites. 17th century